ANGELS AND AGES

ADAM GOPNIK

———

ANGELS
AND
AGES

———

A SHORT BOOK ABOUT
DARWIN, LINCOLN,
AND
MODERN LIFE

ALFRED A. KNOPF, NEW YORK, 2009

THIS IS A BORZOI BOOK
PUBLISHED BY ALFRED A. KNOPF

This book began as two essays that originally appeared in *The New Yorker:*
"Rewriting Nature: Charles Darwin, Natural Novelist" (October 23, 2006) and
"Angels and Ages: Lincoln's Language and Its Legacy" (May 28, 2007).

ISBN-13: 978-1-61523-371-7

Manufactured in the United States of America

For my mother and father—onlie begetters and first professors

CONTENTS

ANGELS AND AGES

ANGELS & AGES

The middleweight champion [of the early twentieth century, Stanley Ketchel] was stunned by [Wilson] Mizner's recitation of the Langdon Smith classic that starts "When you were a tadpole and I was a fish, In the Palaeozoic time" and follows the romance of two lovers from one geological age to another, until they wind up in Delmonico's. Ketchel had a thousand questions about the tadpole and the fish, and Mizner, a pedagogue at heart, took immense pleasure in wedging the whole theory of evolution into the fighter's untutored head. Ketchel became silent and thoughtful. He declined an invitation to see the town that night with Mizner and [Willus] Britt. When they rolled in at 5 a.m., Ketchel was sitting up with his eyes glued on a bowl of goldfish. "That evolution is all the bunk!" he shouted angrily, "I've been watching those fish nine hours and they haven't changed a bit." Mizner had to talk fast; one thing Ketchel couldn't bear was to have anybody cross him.

—Alva Johnston, *The Legendary Mizners*

Americans seemed to fascinate Picasso. Once, in Paris, he invited the Murphys to his apartment, on the Rue de la Boëtie, for an *apéritif,* and, after showing them through the place, in every room of which were pictures in various stages of completion, he led Gerald rather ceremoniously to an alcove that contained a tall cardboard box. "It was full of illustrations, photographs, engravings, and reproductions clipped from newspapers. All of them dealt with a single person—Abraham Lincoln. 'I've been collecting them since I was a child,' Picasso said, 'I have thousands, thousands!' He held up one of Brady's photographs of Lincoln, and said with great feeling, 'There is the real American elegance!' "

—Calvin Tomkins, *Living Well Is the Best Revenge*

We are all pebbles dropped in the sea of history, where the splash strikes one way and the big tides run another, and though what we *feel* is the splash, the splash takes place only within those tides. In almost every case, the incoming current drowns the splash; once in a while the drop of the pebble changes the way the ocean runs. On February 12, 1809, two baby boys were born within a few hours of each other on either side of the Atlantic. One entered life in a comfortable family home, nicely called the Mount, that still stands in the leafy English countryside of Shrewsbury, Shropshire; the other opened his eyes for the first time in a nameless long-lost log cabin in the Kentucky woods. Charles Darwin was the fifth of six children, born into comfort but to a family that was far from "safe," with a long history of free-thinking and radical beliefs. He came into a world of learning and money—one grandfather, Josiah Wedgwood, had made a fortune in ceramic plates. Abraham Lincoln was the second of three, born to a dirt-poor farmer, Thomas Lincoln, who, when he wrote his name at all, wrote it (his son recalled) "bunglingly."

Their narrow circles of immediate experience were held inside that bigger ocean of outlying beliefs and assumptions. In any era, there are truths that people take as obvious, stories that they think are weird or wrong, and dreams that they believe are distant or doomed. (We like stories about time travel and living robots, and even have some speculative thoughts about how they might be made to happen. But on the whole we believe that the time we're living in, and the way we live in it, is just the natural way things are. We *like* strange stories but believe only a few.) The obvious truths of 1809, the kind that were taught in school, involved what could be called a "vertical" organization of life, one in which we imagine a hierarchy of species organized on earth, descending from man on down toward animals, and a judge appraising us up above in heaven. Man was stuck in the middle, looking warily up and loftily down. People mostly believed that the kinds of organisms they saw on earth had always been here and always would be, that life had been fixed in place since the beginning of a terrestrial time, which was thought to go back a few thousand years at most. The eighteenth-century Enlightenment had, of course, already deepened a faith in Reason among the elite, but it was not a popular movement. It had altered many ideas without changing most minds. (John Stuart Mill could say, as late as the 1850s, that he was still almost the only Englishman he knew who had not been brought up as a believer.) The Enlightenment ideal of Reason was in any case bound by taxonomies and hierarchies, absolute and extended right through earth and time. That the long history of life might be one driven by shifting coalitions of contingency, with chance having at least one hand on the reins, was still a mostly unthinkable idea. The forms of life were set, and had never varied. "Species have a real existence in nature, and a transition from one to another does not exist" was the way one magus put it, decisively.

People also believed, using what they called examples ancient and modern—and the example of the Terror in France, which had only very recently congealed into Napoleon's empire, was a strong case—that societies without inherited order were intrinsically weak, unstable, and inclined to dissolve into anarchy or tyranny. Democracy in the sense we mean it now was a fringe ideal of a handful of radicals. Even in America the future of democracy was unclear, in part because of the persistence of slavery, which was still a feature of Western life. Democracy was hard to tell from mob rule and the tyranny of mob rule. Democracy existed, and was armed, but didn't feel entirely liberal; the difference between reformist parliamentary government and true democracy seemed disturbingly large even to well-intentioned people. In the 1830s, Tocqueville, sympathetic to American democracy, was still skeptical about its chances, writing that "until men have changed their nature and been completely transformed, I shall refuse to believe in the duration of a government which is called upon to hold together forty different nations covering an area half that of Europe, to avoid all rivalry, ambition, and struggles between them, and to unite all their independent wills in the accomplishment of common designs." Throughout Europe and America many thoughtful, truth-seeking people also believed in divine judgment and an afterlife in more or less literal terms.

The thought of no time is monolithic, and the people of 1809 in England and America did not believe these things absolutely. The new science of geology was pressing back the history of the earth; old bones would start turning up that threatened old stories; the new textual studies of the Bible were pressing against an easy acceptance of their truth, too. And there were many Utopian radical democrats in both countries. We can find plenty of astonishing ideas in that day, just as we will find traces of the astonishing ideas of the next century somewhere on the fringes of our own time. But on the whole these ideas belonged to the world of what would have been called "fancy," not fact.

By the time Abraham Lincoln and Charles Darwin were dead—the American murdered by a pro-slavery terrorist in 1865, the Englishman after a long illness in 1882—the shape of history had changed, and the lives they had led and the things they had said had done a lot to change it. Two small splashes had helped to move the tide of time. Very different beliefs, ones that we now treat as natural and recognize as just part of the background hum of our time, were in place: the world was understood to be very, very old, and the animals and plants in it were known to have changed dramatically over the aeons—and though just how they had changed was still debated, the best guesses, then as now, involved slow alteration through a competition for resources over a very long time. People were convinced, on the whole, that democratic government, arrived at by reform or revolution, was a plausible and strong way to organize a modern nation—that republican regimes were fighters and survivors. (A giant statue, one of the largest since antiquity, of a goddess of Liberty was under construction in once-again republican France for a vindicated republican America, just to commemorate this belief.) Slavery in the Western world was, for the first time in thousands of years, finished (although racism wasn't). Liberal republicanism and universalist democracy had begun the steady merger that persists to this day, so that most of us no longer see the governing systems of Canada and the United States as decisively, rather than locally, different.

Most of all, people thought that, in one way or another, by some hand or another, the world had changed and would continue to change, that the hierarchies of nature and race and class that had governed the world, where power fell in a fixed chain on down, were false. Fixity was not reality. Life changed, and ways of living changed, too. Life was increasingly lived on what we can think of as a horizontal, with man looking behind only to see what had happened before, and forward to see what he could make next. On that horizontal plane, we are invested in our future as much as in our afterlife, and in our children more than in our ancestors. These beliefs, which we hold still, are part of what we call the modern condition—along with the reactive desire to erase the instability that change brings with it, to get us thinking up and down again, instead of merely back and forth.

The two boys born on the same day to such different lives had become, as they remain, improbable public figures of that alteration of minds—they had become what are now called in cliché "icons," secular saints. They hadn't made the change, but they had helped to midwife the birth. With the usual compression of popular history their reputations have been reduced to single words, mottoes to put beneath a profile on a commemorative coin or medal—"Evolution!" for one and "Emancipation!" for the other. With the usual irony of history, the mottoes betray the men. Lincoln came late—in the eyes of Frederick Douglass, maddeningly late—and reluctantly to emancipation, while perhaps the *least* original thing in Darwin's amazingly original work was the idea of evolution. (He figured out *how* it ran; he took a poetic figure familiar to his grandfathers and put an engine and a fan belt in it.) We're not wrong to work these beautiful words onto their coins, though: the two were the engineers of the alterations. They found a way to make those words live.

Darwin and Lincoln did not make the modern world. But they helped to make our moral modernity. The two little stories at the head of this chapter suggest just how widely their images and ideas had already spread within a half century of their deaths: in the first decade of the last century the concept of evolution troubled and fascinated and intrigued even a middleweight boxer, whose indignation at *not actually seeing it happen* anticipates that of many just-as-two-fisted skeptics today, while Lincoln's face would haunt the imagination of an artist remaking art. For more than a century they've been part of the climate of modern life, systems in the weather of the modern world.

The shared date of their birth is, obviously, "merely" a coincidence, what historians like to call an "intriguing coincidence." But coincidence is the vernacular of history, the slang of memory— the first strong pattern where we begin to search for more subtle ones. Like the simultaneous deaths of Thomas Jefferson and John Adams on July 4, 1826, the accidental patterns of birth and death point to other patterns of coincidence in bigger things. (Jefferson and Adams, born at about the same time, were likely to die at about the same time; that they willed themselves to live long enough to see in the holiday says something about the urgency of the new rituals of the Republic.)

As long ago as the early twentieth century, the shared birthday of Darwin and Lincoln seemed central enough to an idea of liberal democratic civilization to have inspired a proposal for a binational, transatlantic holiday: the birthday of the two, "Lincoln, the embodiment of Anglo-Saxon devotion to Justice, and Darwin, the incarnation of Anglo-Saxon devotion to Truth," should be declared an international holiday, a Massachusetts writer named

William Thayer insisted in 1908, making the rational and good point that Lincoln was exceptional in being without malice, Darwin, in welcoming criticism and argument—though Thayer rather weakens his point, to our minds, by all those "Anglo-Saxon" attitudes. (Useful reminders, really, that similar assumptions, which will seem just as onerous or absurd to our great-grandchildren, linger in the corners of our minds, too.)

My own head has been filled with images and ideas of the two men since I was small. My father introduced me first to Lincoln, pressing on me a picture book called *Meet Mr. Lincoln,* a handsome oversize thing connected to a television special of 1959, filled with black-and-white Brady photographs—and the gravity, the melancholy, the destiny of that face touched me as it has touched so many others. (Readers will recall that Alexander Portnoy, too, was turned on to a lifetime of commitment to human rights, among other human activities, simply by the soulfulness of the statue of Lincoln in downtown Newark, outside the Essex County Court House.) Darwin was my mother's hero, though it would be years before, one summer on a beach, I actually read *On the Origin of Species.* Then I discovered, as have generations of readers since that fateful day in 1859 when the entire first print run sold out in a day, that it is not just a Great Book but a great book, an absorbing, wonderful adventure in argument, a beach read in which your view of the world is changed by the end even if your view of the world was agreeable to it at the beginning. It's a Victorian hallucinogen, where the whole world suddenly comes alive and begins moving, so that the likeness between seagulls and sandpipers on the beach where you are reading suddenly becomes spookily animated, part of a single restless whole, with the birds' giant lizard ancestors looming like ghosts above them. What looks like the fixed, unchanging solitude of the beach and ocean suddenly becomes alive to, vulnerable to, an endless chain of change and movement. It's a book that makes the whole world vibrate.

As I grew older and read more, I began to understand Lincoln and Darwin as symbols of the two pillars of the society we live in: one representing liberal democracy, the other the human sciences—one a faith in armed republicanism and government of the people, the other a belief that objective knowledge about human history and the human condition, who we are and how we got here, exists. This makes them, plausibly, "heroes."

But they are also amazing men, something more than heroes, and the more you read about their lives, the more you're moved by their private struggles as much as by their public acts. Both men are our contemporaries still because they were among the first big men in history who belonged to what is sometimes called "the bourgeois ascendancy." They were both family men. They loved their wives uxoriously, lived for their children, and were proud of their houses. Darwin was born to money, and though he kept some gentry tastes and snobberies, like the royal family of Albert and Victoria, whose reign superintended most of his life, he chose to live his life not in imitation of the old aristocracy but in the manner of the new bourgeoisie—involving his children in every element of his life, having them help with his experiments, writing his autobiography for them, and very nearly sacrificing his chance at history for the love of his religious wife. Lincoln's place in history was won by his rise to the presidency, but his first and perhaps even harder rise was to the big middle-class house and expensive wife he adored. What we wonder at is that a simple Springfield lawyer could become president; from his point of view, probably what was really amazing was that a cabin-born bumpkin had become a Springfield lawyer. Both men were shaped in crucial ways by the worst of nineteenth-century woes, the death of children at the height of their charm and wisdom. The nineteenth century was cruel in that it gave children a chance at a long life and often took it from them—the full force of exceptional grief set against the background of increasing hope for long life. (This is why the saddest scenes in literature, wrongly called sentimental, come to us from that time.)

Both men even had what one might call the symptomatic diseases of middle-class modernity, the kind that our age picks out among the great roll call of human ills to name and obsess over. Lincoln was a depressive; Darwin, subject to anxiety attacks so severe that he wrote down one of the most formidable definitions of a panic attack that exists. Though the source of these ailments—in nature or genes, bugs or traumas—remains mysterious, their presence is part of the two men's familiarity. They had the same domestic pleasures, and the same domestic demons, as we have.

And they are both near-perfect national types: the ugly, direct, plainspoken American, shrewder than he looks and more eloquent than he pretends, a type that every generation since has tried to mimic in its politicians and movie stars, from Harry Truman through Jimmy Stewart and Tom Hanks. That *is* the real American elegance. The Englishman is just as English as the American is American: inward turning, possessed by a family and class loyalty so absolute that it is hardly conscious, genuinely humble but still possessed by a conviction beyond all argument that his nation and class are the chosen people. Fastidious to the point of neurosis, quietly eloquent, fearful of fuss and show, hating showy ideas, people, and art, but with an eccentric corner saved for a particular kind of breathless and innocent love of flamboyance, for the sexual displays of birds and bugs—he is a type reproduced in every British war film, the quiet man who takes the hill without blowing his own bugle, or waiting for another's.

We must be realistic about what they were like: not saints nor heroes nor gods but people. Darwin and Lincoln are admirable and, in their ways, even lovable men. But Lincoln, we have always to remember, was a war commander, who had men shot and boy-deserters hanged after sitting on their coffins in the sun. We would, I think, be taken aback at a meeting. Lincoln summed up in one word was *shrewd,* a backwoods lawyer with a keen sense of human weakness and a knack for clever argument, colder than we would think, and more of a pol and even more of a wise guy than we would like him to be. Winning is the probity of politics, and a good pol is more concerned with winning—elections, cases, and arguments—than with looking noble. Lincoln was smart, shrewd, and ambitious before he was, as he became, wise, farseeing, and self-sacrificing. If we had been around to watch him walk across a room, instead of stride through history, what we would have seen were the normal feet that left the noble prints. Sure of himself even at the worst of the Civil War, he paced the floor, crying out not "What have I done?" but "What will the country say?"

Darwin we would likely find far more frumpy and tedious than we like our heroes to be—one of those naturalists who run on and on narrowly about their pet subjects. He would frown and furrow his brow and make helpless embarrassed harrumphs if any of his fervent admirers arrived today and asked him what he thought of man's innate tendencies to relish Tchaikovsky. One can easily imagine him brought back to earth and forced onto a television-studio platform with eager admirers (like this one) pressing him for his views on sexual equality or the origins of the love of melody in the ancient savanna and becoming more and more unhappy and inarticulate—in his day it was German naturalists; now it would be American journalists, though he had those, too—until at last swallowed up in a vast, sad, melancholy, embarrassed English moan.

Not that Lincoln didn't care about morality, but he cared more about winning, wars and arguments, than about appearing to be a paragon. Not that Darwin wasn't interested in speculative consequences of his theory—he was—but the habit of pontification was completely alien to him, unless it was reassuringly tied with a bow of inductive observation. We are here to treat them philo-sophically, with the strong understanding that neither man was a philosopher, or tried to be.

The framing image, and the title, of this book comes from a dis-pute over the famous epitaph offered at Lincoln's deathbed by his secretary of war, Edwin Stanton: did Stanton say, "Now he belongs to the ages," or "Now he belongs to the angels"? This small historical mystery is one that I set out to solve, but its mean-ing—its echo—lies in what the ongoing dispute says about the two or more sides of Lincoln's placement in the history of faith. Was it natural, inevitable, for someone at Lincoln's deathbed, sur-rounded by his circle, to refer overtly to the mechanism of heaven, as generations had done in respect to the not particularly devout Washington's death, showing his bed lifted to paradise by cherubs? Or would that overt religiosity have been inflected by a reference to time, to fate, to destiny, to history—to the ages?

This dispute dovetailed neatly with the other great dispute of the time, which enmeshed Darwin and reached its most memo-rable form in T. H. Huxley's debate with Bishop Wilberforce, which was distilled by the great Disraeli into a neat epigraph: "Is man an ape or an angel?" ("I am on the side of the angels," Dis-raeli then added with more mischief and irony—coming as the statement did from a famously "diabolical" figure—than we always remember.) Apes or angels: which were human beings to be imagined as descended from? The three terms together make up a small constellation of our symbols. Where did we, human beings, fit among them all? Angels, apes, and ages: old divine agents, the animal past, the force of time—it is the neat trinity that still helps organize our emotions. If we accept the rule of angels, can we deal with the fact of ages? Can we be apes and still be angels? Can we live in ages and not be only apes?

The three terms have oddly never seemed more a part of the general buzz and hum of life than they do right now. We are arguing about these things again. Fifty years ago no one would have chosen Darwin and Lincoln as central figures of the modern imagination. Freud and Marx would perhaps have been the minds that we saw as the princes of our disorder. But with the moral (and lesser intellectual) failure of Marxism, and the intellectual (and lesser moral) failure of Freud, Marx and Freud's ideas have retreated into the history of modernity, among the vast systematic ideas that proposed to explain it all to you.

Lincoln and Darwin, by contrast, have never been more present: Lincoln is the subject of what seems to be the largest biographical literature outside that of Jesus and Napoleon, while Darwin continues not only to cause daily fights but to inspire whole new sciences—or are they pseudo sciences? The irony is that the most radical thing around, at the birth of the new millennium, turned out to be liberal civilization—both the parliamentary, "procedural" liberalism of which Lincoln, for all his inspirational gifts, was an adherent, and the scientific liberalism, the tradition of cautious pragmatic free thought that engaged Darwin, skeptical of grand systems even as science creates them. Science and democracy still look like the hope of the world (even as we recognize that their intersection gave us the means to burn alive every living thing on the planet at will). The marriage of science and democratic politics represents for us liberal civilization, the twinned hopeful note of our time—along with their depressing extension, mass-conscription wars and a stoic acceptance of deep time and pointless mass dying.

The proliferation of writing about both men, in the past decade especially, means that it may be hard for the amateur reader to pick through it all, and I hope to make the job easier. Was Lincoln a Christian? a racist? Was he a capitalist tool, a corporate lawyer first and a man of principle second? How cynically did he practice politics? Why did he delay emancipation (if he did)? With Darwin similar questions arise: Was *he* a racist? a believer? Why did he delay publishing his theory (if he did)? Were his personal ethics actually in keeping with his professed ones? How did he feel about his children? his wife? Without pretending to solve these questions, at least I can offer a sense of the topography, what the lay of the literary land is like right now and who stands in ambush behind the trees. (I ask the forbearance of Lincoln and Darwin scholars in doing this, but scholarship only matters when it makes students of us all.)

Above all, I want to help with the hard, embarrassing, but necessary question, which scholarship, strangely, can pose but can't in its nature help much to resolve: what were they *like*? (I met someone once who had known Einstein. What he was like was all I wanted to know, and the hardest thing for him to tell me.) And deeper questions, too: How do we reconcile the Lincoln who we know was a powerfully good man with the hard commander who knowingly sent thousands of young men to their certain deaths, and kept sending them off after he knew how horribly many of them would die? How was he able to see them as mere arithmetic? And what consolation for life did Darwin find in his own long view of a blind and slow-footed Nature?

In this sense, what makes the two men worth looking at together is that they *aren't* particularly remarkable. The things that intrigued and worried them and made them stay up nights were the same things that most other intelligent people in their day worried about, the same kinds of things that keep us up nights, too. An entire mountain range of minds rises between them and around them, most of the rest submerged by history. But they are high peaks within it, and they look out toward each other. And from on top of one you can see the other. They are still above water because what they made of those worries was something big, a permanent mountain of meaningful anxiety.

Lives lived in one time have similar shapes, and the common shape is itself a subject. I wanted to write about both men because I loved their characters and revered their accomplishments, but also for the most honest of writer's reasons: contemplating them gave me a chance to think at length about other things that matter a lot to me. Yet anyone writing an extended study of two very different men must always be haunted by Fluellen's persuasive comparison, in Shakespeare's *Henry V,* of Henry V and Alexander the Great: "There is a river in Macedon; and there is also moreover a river at Monmouth—it is called Wye at Monmouth, but it is out of my prains what is the name of the other river; but 'tis all one, 'tis alike as my fingers is to my fingers, and there is salmons in both."

There is salmons in both—unearned or, anyway, unpersuasive parallels exist between all lives lived in a time. The positive connections between Darwin and Lincoln are in a way the least interesting thing about pairing them. Which isn't to say that there are *no* neat ties to join them. Though neither had come from slave-owning families, they both, as they grew up, saw enough of slavery to become absolutely opposed to it, a level of revulsion that was unusual even among those who despised the institution. They shared a mutual appreciation of one hugely important, flawed, and mostly forgotten nineteenth-century book, the anonymously published *Vestiges of the Natural History of Creation,* which first appeared in 1844 and gave a theory of evolution, though one without a mechanism or even much biology. (It turned out to have been written by a Scottish writer and publisher named Robert Chambers.) William Herndon, Lincoln's closest friend and one of his first biographers, tells us that the then-freethinking (that is, more or less openly atheist) Lincoln liked this evolutionary idea because of its *causality,* its insistence that everything happened for a discernible reason, from natural, not miraculous, causes. Around the same time, Darwin wrote to Thomas Huxley to compliment his bulldog on his review of *The Vestiges:* "I have just been reading your Review of the Vestiges, & the way you handle a great Professor is really exquisite & inimitable . . . but I cannot think but that you are rather hard on the poor author. I must think that such a book, if it does no other good, spreads the taste for natural science.—But I am perhaps no fair judge for I am almost as unorthodox about species as the Vestiges itself, though I hope not *quite* so unphilosophical."

The real common stuff, and the really significant subject, though, lies at a deeper level—in the kinds of words both men used, and in a new kind of liberal language that they helped to invent. They matter most because they wrote so well. Lincoln's eloquence was public and central: he got to be president mostly because he made a couple of terrific speeches in famous halls, and we revere him above all because he gave a few more as president. Darwin was a writer among scientists and a scientist among writers; though he didn't think he was a natural writer, he published his big ideas in popular books. A commercial publishing house published *On the Origin of Species* along with novels and memoirs, and *The Origin* remains probably the only book that changed science that an amateur reader can still sit down and read right through for pleasure while being told mostly true things. (Galileo's *Dialogue Concerning the Two Chief World Systems* is still fun to read, but his polemic is more dated; he is arguing with Aristotle, not an archbishop.) Above all, *The Origin* is a long argument meant for amateur readers, an effort at popular persuasion. It's so well written that we don't think of it as well written, just as Lincoln's speeches are so well made that they seem to us as natural as pebbles on the beach. (We don't think, "Well said!" We just think, "That's right!")

Writing well isn't just a question of winsome expression, but of having found something big and true to say and having found the right words to say it in, of having seen something large and having found the right words to say it small, small enough to enter an individual mind so that the strong ideas of what the words are saying sound like sweet reason. Good writing is mostly good seeing and good thinking, too. It involves a whole view of life, and making that view sound so plausible that the reader adheres to it as obvious before he knows that it's radical. (Their great contemporary Karl Marx had none of it; his views strike us as radical before we accept them as obvious. It is no accident—as a Marxist would say—that he criticized *both* Darwin and Lincoln for being too mundane and banal as stylists.)

The language they helped invent is still a rhetoric that we respond to—a new style, of persuasion and argument, that belongs to liberalism. (I mean liberalism here, and throughout this book, not in the American sense of well-meaning and wishy-washy, or the French sense of savagely devoted to the free market, but in the British sense, John Stuart Mill's sense, in which an individual is committed, at the same time, to constitutional rule *and* individual freedom, to the power of the many *and* the free play of the mind—the sense that takes in a "conservative" in our politics just as well as a "liberal," if not in a way more.)

One of the great tides of the time they lived in was the one that made the Western world, willy-nilly, more and more democratic, in the simple sense that more and more people knew how to read and reason, and expected to be persuaded to new convictions rather than just policed into them. Lincoln grew up in a society that, though by European standards was in some ways primitive, was richly rhetorical. In backwoods Ohio, in the 1840s, William Dean Howells, Lincoln's campaign biographer, recalled, "The village wits . . . liked to stand with their backs to our stove and challenge opinion concerning Holmes and Poe, Irving and Macaulay, Pope and Byron, Dickens and Shakespeare." Later, the inventions of the telegraph and modern mass journalism would give political words an immediacy that they had never had before. People knew about Lincoln because they knew he had debated Stephen Douglas, and they knew the kinds of arguments he had made and the tone and style he had used to make them.

Darwin, in turn, might have made his ideas public through the narrow channels of professional publication and specialist lectures. But he didn't. He chose to write books that anyone could read, and that almost everyone did read. And though he wasn't a platform man himself, he saw to it that he had good friends who were, and that his big idea got known through popular public debates. He wanted to be right, but he also wanted to be *heard*. (One of the most important acts in the acceptance of Darwinism was a review that appeared not in a scientific journal but in the London *Times* just after *The Origin*'s publication.)

The style they found to get heard was a new one, and one they shared. They were nearsighted visionaries. They knew how to inspire, but they knew how to argue first. They *particularized* in everything, and their general vision rises from the details, their big ideas from small sightings. Lincoln's provisos, his second thoughts, his lawyerliness, are as impressive as his prophecies, while Darwin's observational obsessions are what made his big idea live. Good writers have always argued from facts, but few before had taken such narrow paths of reason toward the broad road of truth. They shared logic as a form of eloquence, argument as a style of virtue, close reasoning as a form of uplift. Each, using a form of technical language—the fine, detailed language of natural science for Darwin, the tedious language of legal reasoning for Lincoln—arrived at a new ideal of liberal eloquence. This was a revolution in rhetoric that we still live with, and within, rhetoric remade by a suspicion of rhetoric.

In the past decades, through the work of historians like Garry Wills in America and Gillian Beer in England, we've come to have a better idea of how both men turned their ideas into words. But thinking of them in counterpoint helps us see something more than we can see by looking at either of them alone, and that is the way a particular rhetoric, a particular power and style of speech, goes hand in hand with the ascendancy of a certain kind of secular liberalism. Theirs was the kind of liberal talk that values eloquence as a form of reticence, and regards argument itself as the point—as transcendence rather than as instrument. The way that Darwin uses madly detailed technical arguments about the stamen of an orchid to make, many, many pages later, a vast cosmic point about the nature of survival and change on the planetary time scale, and the way that Lincoln uses lawyerly arguments about who signed what when among the Founders to make the case for war, if necessary, to end slavery—these styles have in common the writer's faith in plain English, his hope that people's minds and hearts can be altered by the slow crawl of fact as much as by the long reach of revelation.

Snails with sublime purposes are what they both were, and they saw the rabbits and hummingbirds of oratory by repetition and argument by insistence, like that of the author of the *Vestiges*— who rushed to the end without going slowly over the ground— as leftovers, unserious contenders for ideas that could be won only painful inch by painful inch. (In Lincoln's case, these painful inches became all too real, as the battlegrounds of war.) Our idea of eloquence—which includes a suspicion of too much of it— begins here. There's a lovely story told by Herndon about Lincoln's laughing at the kind of alliterative, orotund eloquence that was dying in his time. Darwin's impatience with Chambers was not an impatience with the radical thought—he thought Chambers was not radical enough—but with his trying to make hard points in easy ways. When Darwin said he wanted to be more philosophical than Chambers, he meant nearly the opposite of what we would mean now: not more abstract and general and elevated, but more specific and exact and argumentative. The often mysterious poetry of their words—"disenthrall ourselves," "the better angels of our nature," "the mystic chords," "this view of life"—haunts us because it is set against a background of willfully unpoetic and even anti-poetic speech. They built their inspiration from induction; their phrases still ring because they were struck on bells cast of solid bronze, not on chimes blowing in the breeze. The replacement of the romantic love of imagination and honor with the romance of observation and argument—that was the heart of who they were, and what they gave to us.

In the long run, it is not what they have in common with each other that matters; it is what they have in common with *us*. We live in a society based on two foundations, scientific reasoning and democratic politics, and their offspring, technology and prosperity. (We know technology to be the offspring of science, and we believe, at least, that widespread abundance is the result of liberty doing its work in markets and minds alike.) Lincoln showed, to a degree that we no longer understand, that democratic politics were compatible with long-term survival—or, to put it bluntly, with military victory, winning armies. (The French army had begun to win big only after it lost its republican character.) Darwin showed that scientific reasoning could explain not only the life of matter but the matter of life; it could come up with a plausible theory of the history of life on this planet, which until then had seemed as mysterious as the birth of time seems to us now. The immediate gain of science is machines; the immediate gain of democracy is money. Ours is a society whose two pillars—science and democracy, an idea of objective knowledge arrived at by skepticism and of liberty available to all—have given us the A-bomb, the H-bomb, mass alienation: the most peaceful and prosperous and tolerant societies that the world has ever seen, which balance on the brink of total global annihilation every day.

This is a study in a new kind of eloquence, and a new kind of life the new eloquence spoke to. The subject is liberal civilization and its language—the way we live now and the way we talk at home and in public. These are essays without an agenda, but this is not a book without a thesis. The thesis is that literary eloquence is essential to liberal civilization; our heroes should be men and women possessed by the urgency of utterance, obsessed by the need to see for themselves and to speak for us all. Authoritarian societies can rely on an educated elite; mere mass society, on shared dumb show. Liberal cities can't. A commitment to persuasion is in itself a central liberal principle. New ways of thinking demand new kinds of eloquence. Our world rests on science and democracy, on seeing *and* saying; it rests on thinking new thoughts and getting them heard by a lot of people. Oratory, as Pericles knew, was what mattered crucially to the first democracy, in fifth-century B.C. Athens, but that was a small affair of few citizens (and many slaves) compared with our own, which needs words of all kinds, written and spoken and shouted, coming at you from all directions.

The point is not that writing well is a proof of thinking clearly. Orwell was wrong about that, sadly. The truth is that plenty of men who have written very well have thought horrible thoughts, and the thoughts have been made to seem less horrible by being well written. No, the point is that when we do come across those who write well *and* see clearly, we're right to make them heroes.

Or even more. These two princes—call them prophets, why not?—of liberal civilization, of a world without a present God but with providential purposes, of justifying ages more than ministering angels, may shine light on the kind of place we've made, and the way we can make it better. By disputing with the angels, they helped to begin our age—but by the judgment of the ages, were they really on the side of the angels all along?

CHAPTER ONE

LINCOLN'S MIND

A DEATHBED MYSTERY

A HISTORICAL DISPUTE, A DEEPER PLAY

FROM LAST WORDS TO FIRST WORDS

A BOY BORN TO READ—AND WRITE

THE FRONTIER, LAND OF A THOUSAND RHETORICAL STYLES

WHY HE CHOSE THE LAW

HIS RISE TO THE BAR,
HIS MARRIAGE, AND HIS HOUSE

A GENERAL PRACTITIONER OF LAW

LEGAL STYLES OF ARGUMENT, LAW AND LANGUAGE

1838 LYCEUM SPEECH: REASON ALONE

ONE-SYLLABLE REDUCTIONS;
SAY IT FANCY, SAY IT PLAIN

A SOURCE IN SHAKESPEARE

LINCOLN AND RACE • FOR LAW, AGAINST HONOR

JOHN BROWN, THE ANTI-LINCOLN

THE CODE OF HONOR, NORTH AND SOUTH

AN APPARENT DEFICIT • LINCOLN'S ONE SAD DUEL

WEAK TEA AND STRONG WHISKEY

LEGAL ARGUMENT AS LIBERAL ELOQUENCE

Begin, then, with the angels, and the ages, and the argument. On the morning of April 15, 1865, Abraham Lincoln, president and victor, lay dying from a bullet that had lodged in his skull just behind his right eye. At 7:22 a.m., as Lincoln drew his last breath, all the worthies who had crowded into a little back bed-room in a boardinghouse across the street from Ford's Theatre turned to Edwin Stanton, Lincoln's formidable secretary of war, for a final word.

Stanton is the one with the long comic beard and the spinster's spectacles, who in the photographs looks a bit like Mr. Pickwick but was actually the iron man in the cabinet and who, after a difficult beginning, had come to revere Lincoln as a man and a writer and a politician—had even played something like watchful Horatio to his tragic Hamlet. Stanton stood still, sobbing, and then—according to every biography of Lincoln from Nicolay and Hay's to Doris Kearns Goodwin's—said, simply, "Now he belongs to the ages."

It's probably the most famous epitaph in American biography, and still perhaps the best. The words seem perfectly chosen in their bare and stoic evocation of a Lincoln who belongs to history alone, their invocation not of an assumption to an afterlife but of a long reign in the corridors of time, of a man now part of eternity.

Yet in recent years, it has become possible to find an entirely different version of that sentence. In Jay Winik's *April 1865* and in James L. Swanson's *Manhunt,* for instance, the reader once again comes to the deathbed scene, the vigil, the gathering. Swanson writes that the Reverend Dr. Gurley, the Lincoln family minister, said,

> "Let us pray." He summoned up . . . a stirring prayer. . . .
> Gurley finished and everyone murmured "Amen."
> Then, no one dared to speak.
> Again Stanton broke the silence. "Now he belongs to the angels."

Now he belongs to the angels? Where has *that* come from? you wonder. There is a Monty Python element here ("What was that?" "I think it was 'Blessed are the cheese makers,' " the annoyed listeners too far from the Mount say to each other in *Life of Brian*), but is there something more going on as well? Certainly one can glimpse, just visible beneath the diaphanous middle of the references, the tracings of an ideological difference. Stanton's words as they are normally quoted are (like the Lincoln Memorial) a form of American neoclassicism, typical of the American liberal estimation of Lincoln as an essentially secular hero and at odds with the figure of Christian nobility prized by the right: Lincoln's afterlife lies not in heaven but in his vindication by history.

Does he belong to the angels or to the ages? This small implicit dispute echoes, in turn, a genuine historical debate: between those historians who insist on a tough Lincoln, the Lincoln whom Edmund Wilson, in *Patriotic Gore,* saw as an essentially Bismarckian figure—a cold-blooded nationalist who guaranteed the unity of the American nation, a stoic emperor in a stovepipe hat whose essential drive was for power, his own and his country's—and those who, like Sandburg and Goodwin, see a tender, soulful Lincoln, a figure of almost saintly probity and patience, who ended slavery, deepened in faith as the war went on, and fought hard without once succumbing to hatred. A Lincoln for the ages and a Lincoln for the angels already exists. Now the two seem to be at war for his epitaph.

We have to go deep into the odd corners of Lincoln literature to find out what really was said at that pregnant moment. There is an answer out there—or as close to an answer as you can find. Yet even to guess at what was said then, and to have a larger sense of what was meant by Stanton and understood by his listeners—and all those distant, vicarious listeners who have read the words since—we need to understand what words were right for Lincoln. We need to know something about Lincoln's language and its legacy—where the words came from, how he used them, what they meant and, sometimes, didn't mean. Lincoln was a man of strong sentences and strategic silences; looking within them can help to locate him.

Let's postpone the pursuit of the small specific mystery, for a little while at least, to pursue the larger related question, mysterious in its own way, of how a backwoods lawyer became one of the great American writers, how Lincoln made words, and used them, in the years that led to what the Lincoln scholar Harold Holzer has called that "rubber room"—because it seems to expand and contract according to the number of people who claimed to be there—that last sad bed, with angels hovering symbolically above, or ages waiting solemnly beyond.

All wars over Lincoln become wars over his words. In books published in the past two years alone, you can read about Lincoln's "sword" (his writing) and his "sanctuary" (the Soldiers' Home, just outside Washington, where he spent summers throughout the war). There have long been debates, natural in an age before sound recording, over what had actually been said at any given moment by Lincoln or someone in his circle and what people thought they had heard. Even with the Gettysburg Address, despite our possession of what seem to be two drafts and what are certainly several later copies in Lincoln's own hand, there are many arguments about exactly what Lincoln said. Gabor Boritt, in his book *The Gettysburg Gospel,* has a thirty-page appendix that compares what Lincoln (probably) read at the memorial with what people heard and reported. Most of the differences are small and due to understandable confusions—"the world will little note, nor long remember what we say here" became in some reports "the world will little heed what we say here"—or to impatience on the part of a reporter—the *Centralia Sentinel,* of Lincoln's home state, wanting nothing to do with fancy talk, had the speech begin simply "ninety years ago."

A few disputes seem more significant. The *Cincinnati Daily Gazette,* a Republican paper, made the famous first sentence end "that all mankind are created free and equal by a good God," though it's hard to know whether its reporter had deliberately italicized the point or was simply hearing it with his heart. Also in the first sentence, Lincoln's remark that the nation was "conceived in Liberty" was reported in some newspapers as "consecrated to liberty," a more religious reading of the intended message, and there are those who believe that Lincoln made an impromptu alteration. Many reporters heard Lincoln say "this nation, under God, shall have a new birth of freedom," though the phrase "under God" occurs in neither draft of the text; Lincoln may have spontaneously inserted it—a sign of his growing religious consciousness during the last year of the war. In *Lincoln's Sword,* Douglas L. Wilson worries his way through the possibility, preserved in one of the drafts, that Lincoln referred not to "government of the people, by the people," and so on, but to "*this* government of the people, by the people," deliberately circumscribing the meaning.

It is not hard to see, in this exegetical exactitude, something that recalls the attention that scholars give to fine-point disputes about the words and tales of Jesus and his apostles. This attention to verbal minutiae extends to the secondary figures in the Lincoln gospel, as it does to those in Jesus's gospel, even to Lincoln's Judas-Herod figure, John Wilkes Booth. Booth either did or did not say right before, just as, or shortly after he murdered the president, "*Sic semper tyrannis,*" the motto on the state flag of Virginia. Possibly he cried, "The South is avenged!" or "Revenge for the South," and he cried this in the box, or on the stage, or paired with another cry. Of the forty or so reliable witnesses to the assassination whose accounts are collected in Timothy S. Good's *We Saw Lincoln Shot,* some sixteen heard the Latin or the English, only four heard both, and many said that they didn't hear the assassin say anything at all.

Two witnesses heard Booth say, "I have done it!" Well, which was it? It is possible that he said only "*Sic semper tyrannis,*" onstage or off, and that the words were easily misheard by a stunned audience as "The South is avenged." On the other hand, he may have cried out both and then added the gloating remark as he fled. But then why hadn't more people heard him?

Booth himself, for whom the assassination was, as Swanson says, a kind of diabolical work of performance art, insisted on the "right" reading. "I shouted *Sic semper* before I fired," he wrote a few days later in his own note, which he intended to be sent to the newspapers. One of the more pathetic-horrific aspects of the assassination was how desperate Booth was to read his notices in the next day's papers. Having tailored his performance to what he believed would be a shrewd public appeal—even Northerners would have doubts about Lincoln's absolutist claims to power— he was shocked to find that he had canonized a saint and been cast as a villain. (One of the odd things in American history is that we are inclined to "psychologize" acts of assassination that, whatever dark corner of the psyche they are torn from, are clearly and explicitly political in motive. Oswald shot Kennedy in an act of terrorism on behalf of Castro; Sirhan Sirhan killed Bobby Kennedy because he believed him to be pro-Israel; Booth killed Lincoln because Booth was a violent racist who thought that Lincoln would enfranchise blacks and that if he was dead this would be less likely to happen—as, indeed, it turned out to be.)

And then there are the larger, less word-quibbling arguments over Lincoln's language. What did he mean by "disenthrall"? How angelic are "the better angels of our nature"? Who strikes those mystic chords of memory? What is the sense of "And the war came"? Did he say "this nation under God," and if he did, was he being conventional or pointed? And how does one reconcile his 1862 statement "If I could save the Union without freeing *any* slave I would do it" with his later "if slavery is not wrong, nothing is wrong"?

The tendency to obsess over single words and phrases reflects, in part, the semi-divine status of Lincoln in American history. It also reflects the strange shape of his public life. As it was for Jesus, the frame of action is limited, and its climax tragic—scarcely four years at the center of things and then a martyr's death. With long-lived figures, enough evidence, argument, apology, autobiography, memoir, and frail old-age memories usually emerge to blur an image into being—like a television picture, most of our visions of big men and women are made up of countless tiny lines and points of information and utterance emitted over a lifetime, shimmering and flickering together to give us at least the illusion of a fixed image. But with Lincoln, as with Jesus, the time frame is so short, and the words so concise, that we can master nearly the whole of the body of speeches and parables. Yet for all the brevity and lucidity, we can't master the meaning of it all—there is something cryptic, still insufficiently explained, about the arc of the life. The lives are lucid and mysterious at the same time.

The obsessive attention given to each utterance also reflects a desire to show that what he said was as essential to the meaning of his life (as again with Jesus) as were his orders and actions. Lincoln is less a figure made up of blended lines than one made up of a few key statements; he is, almost literally, a man of words. The Lincoln literature, bigger than any other, is also more literary in its focus on what academics call "rhetoric"—not just what someone says but the style with which he says it. In the past twenty-five years, and particularly since the publication of Garry Wills's *Lincoln at Gettysburg,* language and its uses have become a central Lincoln subject. (Wills, preceded by, among others, Van Wyck

Brooks, has been followed by, among others, Alfred Kazin and Douglas Wilson.)

Lincoln *was* a man of his words. The first thing from his hand was a bit of doggerel verse, which he wrote, neatly, in a school-book when he was about eleven:

> *Abraham Lincoln*
> *his hand and pen*
> *he will be good but*
> *god knows When*

Those words are, the scholars tell us, probably not original, one of those bits of schoolboy doggerel that nobody teaches and everyone learns (although no one has found any just like it, and Lincoln, young and old, loved to write rhymes, verse—so maybe the joke *was* his own). But more to the matter, they are a reminder of the single most important thing about the young Lincoln that we know: he loved to read and write.

There is no greater divide in life than the one between kids for whom the experience of learning to read is a painful or tedious one, whose rewards are remote if real, and those for whom the experiences of reading and writing are addictive, entrancing, overwhelming, and so intense as to offer a new life of their own—those for whom the moment of learning to read begins a second life of letters as rich as the primary life of experience. Lincoln was as clear a case of that kind of child, and man, as anyone who has ever lived. His hand and pen were the axis of his existence even as he made his living, and his reputation, first from his body and later with his mouth. He lived to read, and the distaste that still shocks us a little in his attitude toward his father—that Tom wrote his name "bunglingly" still offended his steady-handed son years later—surely has its root in this simple cause. It wasn't that his father could barely read or write; it was that Tom failed to see the point of it for his son, couldn't see that it not only had what then was called "pecuniary value" but also had life purpose. "His hand and pen"—more than his mind and voice, more even than his heart and soul—*are* Lincoln, the reading mind turning the page, the writing fingers adding to the sum of the world's words. The irony, arresting and in a way poignant, is that Lincoln, a man of action—often murderous, uniquely decisive—was first of all a man of books and thoughts and a rueful humorist of their inability to mend men's ways, including his own. He *would* be good, though, and God, or Providence, or fate, or merely the contingencies of history—it took him a lifetime to make up his mind which it was to be, and perhaps he never did—alone knew when.

Lincoln, all his biographers agree, felt most alive as a boy when he was reading. Growing up in rural Indiana, in a society still largely illiterate, he fell on words as other boys fell on sweets. "Abe read all the books he could lay his hands on," his beloved stepmother, Sarah Lincoln, who raised him after the death of his mother, recalled after his martyrdom, "and when he came across a passage that struck him he would write it down on boards if he had no paper and keep it there till he did get paper." Most lists of what he read then fall on the obvious candidates, the schoolroom texts that his relatively well educated stepmother had brought with her to her marriage: *The Pilgrim's Progress* and *Aesop's Fables* and Benjamin Franklin's autobiography. But he absorbed as well a great deal of poetry, and he loved to repeat lugubrious bits of it for his friends. He even seems to have written and published a lugubrious poem in the *Sangamo Journal* and later sent a friend some samples of the kind of verse he liked to write, which, though not exactly Emily Dickinson, have a certain surprising sadness and feel for the power of monosyllables that would later help him in his speechmaking. ("My child-hood home I see again, / And gladden with the view; / And still as mem'ries crowd my brain, / There's sadness in it too—")

In describing the style that he absorbed from all that reading and writing, we always talk about "clarity" and "simplicity." That makes some sense. Talking to a Connecticut minister on a train in 1860, Lincoln is purported to have said that "among my earliest recollections I remember how, when a mere child, I used to get irritated when anybody talked to me in a way I could not understand." Ever since, he had struggled to put each thought "in language plain enough, as I thought, for any boy I knew to comprehend." But *every* prose style is thought to be lucid by the stylist; even fancy poetic manners are thought to give the gift of clarifying metaphor. Both Dr. Johnson's "nodosities" and E. B. White's faux-naïf appeal to clarity and simplicity. (Clarity and simplicity are like naturalness and the return to the classical that occur every year in women's fashion—every mode, no matter how outlandish, appeals to them. Short skirts are liberating, and so are long, the fitted bodice emphasizes a woman's natural lines, and the flowing tunic frees her to move as she likes, naturally.)

All good styles are lucid, but each is lucid in its own way, and in a way shaped by the sounds of its time. We admire Lincoln for being so literary, but when we say that Lincoln was a great writer, it isn't his poetry we're thinking of; it's his speeches. He was a great writer whose form was talking. That was natural. The frontier–Southern fringe society in which he was growing up was, first to last, a rhetorical society, and an oratorical society. Most periods have a manner or style or form that's primary to the way the people of the time organize their feelings about the world. Stephen Greenblatt has shown us how much Elizabethan England was a theatrical society, one in which the pageantry of public life, the ambiguous rituals of religion, even the horrific public executions, flowed in some way into a shared vision of the world as stage.

The frontier America of Lincoln's youth was first of all a rhetorical society, where the ability to speak in public, at length, was central to social ambitions; giving a speech in 1838 in Illinois was the equivalent of putting on a play in 1598 in London, the thing you did into which everything else flowed. (We are, by turn—and a writer says it with sadness—essentially a society of images: a viral YouTube video, an advertising image, proliferates and sums up our desires; anyone who can't play the image game has a hard time playing any public game at all.)

The two most prominent strains of rhetoric that ran through the period and the place were the biblical and the classical; they remained so well into the years of the Civil War. Reading Edward Everett's Gettysburg address, the two-hour set speech that preceded Lincoln's and was meant to be the real event of the Gettysburg commemoration, one is startled to see how relentlessly classical it is in tone and analogy: Everett goes on and *on* about Marathon and the Greeks and the Persian invasions in order to "elevate" Gettysburg and the Union soldiers. Lincoln's rhetoric is, instead, deliberately biblical. (It is difficult to find a single obviously classical reference in any of his speeches.) Lincoln, in turn, had mastered the sound of the King James Bible so completely that he could recast abstract issues of constitutional law in biblical terms, making the proposition that Texas and New Hampshire should be forever bound by a single post office sound like something right out of Genesis.

But though those two—the biblical and the classical—were bedrock, it was a society full of sounds. Mark Twain, whose books give us a better sense of the background to Lincoln's language than any other—William Dean Howells did not call Twain "the Lincoln of our literature" for nothing—shows this as well as anyone. Part of the joy of reading *Huck Finn* is that it's an encyclopedia of the rhetorical styles in small frontier communities before the Civil War: the debased Shakespearean of the Duke and the

Dauphin, the evangelical faux piety of the widow and the judge, orotund and periodic, the genuinely funny tall-tale hyperbole of pap Finn giving it to the govment—a huge range of talk, inflected by Walter Scott at one moment and by classical learning at another, the whole given the necessary gravel of folk obscenity and tall tale.

Part of Lincoln's gift as a speaker was an ability to run easily from one of these dialects to another. He could use both Petroleum Nasby and Shakespeare as references; he is said to have recast Balzac in terms of local people. We all have this gift to one degree or another—it is nearly all that's meant by social skill, and Lincoln was socially skilled; he knew how to make people like him.

Of all those kinds and ways of speaking, though, the one that Lincoln used most often in his oratory was that of close-reasoned legal argument. Lincoln was a lawyer before he was anything else, politician or saint or commander in chief. If in the past decades we've learned a lot about Lincoln's language, the past few years have helped us see Lincoln as a legal man. Brian R. Dirck and Julie M. Fenster, among others, have given a newly sharp picture of Lincoln as traveling lawyer on the Illinois circuit.

Seen from outside, Lincoln's legal years were a preparation for his destiny; seen from inside, Lincoln's years as a lawyer were his life. Every life felt from inside is an epic; for Lincoln, seen from outside, the epic quality comes with the presidency and the war. But from inside it was the rise to the law, and to the bourgeois comfort that the law offered, that was the event of his existence. The real ascent of Lincoln is not only from log cabin to White House; it is from backwoods to the bar. Despite all that childhood reading, he had come perilously close to spending his life as a manual laborer. After he settled in New Salem, Illinois, in 1831, he flirted with becoming a blacksmith before an unsuccessful spell as a small storekeeper led him to the more mind-centered world of deputy to the county surveyor.

In those days, before the guild mentality had taken the professions by the throat, it was still possible to make yourself a lawyer rather than being made one by a professional school. Lincoln did. Between 1831 and 1836, he did the reading that you had to do to pass the bar exam—he seems to have mastered Blackstone's *Commentaries,* hardly a day's work—and set himself up as a practicing lawyer in Springfield, the county seat. The law then was more like real estate now, a profession you started out in early and learned from the ground up. So without "formal" training—with nothing but a lot of reading—Lincoln became a practicing lawyer before he was thirty and soon one of the most admired in his state.

In the old hagiography, Lincoln the lawyer was a fiery, folksy fighter against injustice; to more recent, disillusioned revisionists, he was a corporate lawyer, a "railroad" lawyer doing the work of the new industrialists. The new scholarship shows that both accounts are overdrawn. (Lincoln did do some well-paid work for the railroads, but he took on cases against their interests too.) The bulk of his legal work, which took up the bulk of his professional life, was the predictable work of a small-town lawyer with a wide practice: property disputes, petty criminal cases, family arguments over money, neighbor at war with neighbor, bankruptcies, and, oddly, libel suits in which local women defended themselves against charges of prostitution. His practice was the legal equivalent of a small-town doctor's, treating head colds, lice, scarlet fever, and a rare case or two of venereal disease.

What he learned was not faith in a constant search for justice but the habit of empathetic detachment. The "grease" is what the lawyers of his time called all the lubricants of the law—conciliation, backroom deals, plea bargaining—that allowed conflict to be minimized and trials to be avoided. When we look closely even at the height of the Civil War, Brian Dirck says, "we can see Lincoln the President trying hard to apply a lawyer's grease to the shrill machinery of war." But Lincoln's magnanimity, which was real, began in his work as an Illinois lawyer and should not, Dirck says, be "sentimentalized as a form of kindliness. . . . His magnanimity was also a function of his lawyerly sense of distance from other people's motives, and his appreciation—honed by decades of witnessing nearly every imaginable form of strife in Illinois's courtrooms—of the value of reducing friction as much as possible." The lack of vindictiveness that Lincoln displayed (his favorite expression, his secretary John Hay once explained, was "I am in favor of short statutes of limitations in politics") was the daily requirement of a small-town lawyer. Lincoln believed in letting go; his magnanimity was more strategic than angelic.

But it's also apparent that Lincoln loved the law because he loved the life it led to. Although as a campaign stunt he allowed the image of himself as a rail-splitter to overwhelm the reality of his role as a shrewd expensive practicing lawyer, there can't be any doubt that this boy who had always loved talking and, despite his strength, disliked manual labor was ambitious for a middle-class existence. The law got him a life; the grease got him the goods. Before Lincoln was ambitious for equality, or power, or even prestige, he was ambitious to be a professional man with a big house and a happy family. There are no more telling pictures of Lincoln than those that show him standing on the porch of his big frame house at Eighth and Jackson—bought in 1844, greatly enlarged in 1856—in Springfield. They are the least "Lincoln-like" of all the portraits, not the grave martyr of the nation but a tall man with enough money to build a big house and be proud of it. (Poor boys count their houses by the number of windows they contain; his had seventeen!) His marriage to Mary Todd, for all the erotic passion and cryptic melancholia that ran between them, was first of all a hypergamous marriage—he was marrying up, into a higher-class family than a Kentucky hardscrabble boy could ever have expected to end up in.

Lincoln was a man of a house and a marriage and a family. The Lincolns lived well—by the standards of the day, very well, and by the standards of a boy from the backwoods who, as poor boys don't, had never forgotten his poverty, it must have seemed impossibly well. Daniel Mark Epstein recently composed a loving and funny inventory of all the furniture and accessories that filled the Springfield house: globes of the world and the stars above, three-branch candlesticks and French porcelain pitchers, mirrors with curved legs in gilt frames. It was a Biedermeier idea of heaven, of the kind that was spreading throughout Europe and America at the time.

It was, as well, a place made for a family. In an age when children came increasingly in twos and threes and fours instead of eights and nines and tens, and when there was a reasonable chance that a child who survived the first uncertain years would thrive long after, the attachment of parents to children and, for the first time in a long time, of fathers to children, was very real and very important. Lincoln was away, by the account of his oldest son, Robert, too much of the time, on the circuit arguing cases or else out making speeches. But when he was home, perhaps to overcompensate, he was *home;* there are no more appealing images of Lincoln than those of him playing with and spoiling his children—spoiling them to the point where the Lincolns' lax child-rearing methods became a *schande* among the neighbors. He carried them on his shoulders, held their hands as they danced him down the street, let them run riot in his law office. There is no surer cure for a melancholy man than the presence of small children, and it was a cure that Lincoln took whenever, and as often as, he could (a joy that did not accompany that other cure, the mercury pills that, it is now argued persuasively, he treated himself with in order to cure what he imagined was an incipient case of syphilis).

In one way, then, Lincoln learned in the law, and always kept, a sense that it is better to avoid an argument if you can. But his ambitions remained, as they had always been, fiercely political, and one of the things he found in the law was a new style of political argument.

In politics and on the stage, rhetoric and persuasion are usually essentially the same thing. Say it neatly and make them nod. But in the law, rhetoric and argument sit in constant tension. Eloquence is part of what a lawyer needs, but he also learns, both as a way of preparing for the judge and as a way of impressing the jury, what is in some ways the opposite of eloquence: the close crawl across the facts of a case, the enumerating and deliberating and even pettifogging case making that keeps the law so exasperating and opaque to nonlawyers. And it was the law that Lincoln chose, and though he practiced with occasional bursts of eloquence, most of what we know about his practice suggests that he was as good at the dull procedural part as at the wound-up rug-chewing part, and probably better.

It is the addition of this kind of law talk to high talk that makes Lincoln's rhetoric special. What strikes a newcomer to Lincoln's speeches is how rare those famous cadences are; their simple resonant language—"with malice towards none; with charity for all," the opening and concluding lines of the Gettysburg Address—is memorable in part because there isn't much of it. The majority of Lincoln's public utterances are narrowly, sometimes brilliantly lawyerly—even, on occasion, crafted to give an appearance of inevitability to oratorical conclusions that are not well supported by the chain of reasoning that precedes them. The undramatic small-print language in which Lincoln offered the Emancipation Proclamation is the most famous instance of his mastery of anti-heroic rhetoric. (Karl Marx said that it reminded him of "ordinary summonses sent by one lawyer to another.")

That was what it was meant to sound like. The rhetorical disjunction between the windup and the pitch was part of the performance. Lincoln believed in narrow legalism because he believed that legalism wasn't narrow. The attempt is made, frequently, to explain away these dull, odd, disjointed phrases, but the habit of legal argument—with its tedium and its hairsplitting and even its dubious distinctions and special pleading—is part of Lincoln's rhetoric too.

Lincoln's sense of legal argument as the foundation of liberal eloquence worked itself out over time, but it was at the center of his mind from the beginning. In his first important public speech, the Address Before the Young Men's Lyceum, in Springfield in 1838, Lincoln declared a radical insistence on "reason" to be the only acceptable form of public discourse, the cure for the prevalence and epidemic of violence in American life.

Lincoln was arguing for something, but above all he was arguing *against* something, and that was the code of honor that insisted that a higher law lay outside mere procedural obedience. It is hard now to grasp the cultural authority that the code of passionate honor—with its elaborate rituals of feuds and duels—held in the period, and the primacy that it seemed to give to the South. Not merely the political edge but the poetic priority seemed to lie with the feudal and honorable South against the commercial and mouthy North. (It was a cultural advantage that persisted right up through, and perhaps beyond, the Atlanta premiere of *Gone with the Wind*.)

It was the toleration, even the admiration, that this extralegal code inspired, with its violent consequences for public life, that the young Lincoln set out, ambitiously, to end. He begins by asking, presciently, what threat one might expect to see to American "political institutions," the republican rules passed on by the Founders. Only one thing, he says, has that potential, and it has "pervaded the country," springing up "among the pleasure hunting masters of Southern slaves, and the order loving citizens of the land of steady habits." That thing is uncontrolled violence, set off by mass emotion and intended to end debate. Reviewing

recent "horror-striking" scenes of lynch law and mob violence—
gamblers hanged, Negroes murdered, "a mulatto man, by the
name of McIntosh, . . . seized in the street, dragged to the sub-
urbs of the city, chained to a tree, and actually burned to death;
and all within a single hour from the time he had been a free-
man. . . . Such are the effects of mob law"—Lincoln insisted that
salvation for America lay only in extreme proceduralism, in obeying laws as though they were religious diktats:

> Let every American, every lover of liberty, every well
> wisher to his posterity, swear by the blood of the Revo-
> lution, never to violate in the least particular, the laws of
> the country; and never to tolerate their violation by
> others. . . . Let reverence for the laws, be breathed by
> every American mother, to the lisping babe, that prattles
> on her lap—let it be taught in schools, in seminaries,
> and in colleges;—let it be written in Primmers, spelling
> books, and in Almanacs. . . . And, in short, let it become
> the *political religion* of the nation.

The emphasis, like the passion, is in the original.

Many familiar Lincolnian ironies are in embryo here: the passionate assertion of the dispassionate case for legalism—"never to
violate in the least particular," a tall order for a frontier people—
and absolutist morality and authoritarian legalism seen not as
conflicting but as complementary. The end of the law is to reconcile different interests and let them live together without undue
fanaticism—and everyone should have a fanatic attachment to
that end.

Lincoln then goes on to make a subtle argument for the new
political principle. Emotion *does* play a role in political life; ideas
of sacred honor and moral ideals not yet embodied in law do
count, or, rather, they did count once—they were part of the

invention of the country, not part of its perpetuation: "Passion has helped us; but can do so no more. It will in future be our enemy. Reason, cold, calculating, unimpassioned reason, must furnish all the materials for our future support and defence."

Most students of the Lyceum speech see it as apprentice work, interesting chiefly because it suggests the possibility of a kind of democratic dictator, a giver of rules, as a not entirely displeasing possibility to the young Lincoln. But there is more to the speech than that; the originality lies in the radicalism of its case for reason. Lincoln's argument was simple but original: the curse of American life was violence; its cure was law. Although Lincoln was a Southerner, nothing could be more remote from the Southern cult of honor or idea of noble vengeance. Cold calculation, the dispassionate parsing of the people of the Northern land of steady habits, was the path to the future.

Lincoln tempered but never really abandoned that conviction. His rhetorical genius lay in making cold calculation look like passionate idealism, in making closely reasoned argument ring with the sound of religious necessity. The forces of reason are to be brought in not merely to restrain, curb, and make acceptable the forces of emotion and popular feeling; they must also replace popular emotion—*all* the materials for our future support and defense. The job of the American generation is to make the dull procedures of a law-abiding land—coming to court, obeying summonses, accepting compromises, paying traffic tickets, and doing jury duty—seem as noble and inspiring as the old dreams of revolution and remaking the world.

The traces of this position remain even in Lincoln's great mature speeches. There is, most often, in them a subtle disjunction between his content and his codas, as James Oakes puts it in his fine new account of Lincoln's friendship with Frederick Douglass, *The Radical and the Republican*. The first two-thirds of the speech that Lincoln delivered at Cooper Union in New York in February of 1860 and is generally thought to have made him president—it turned him from a local to a national figure—is, as Harold Holzer has shown, devoted to a maniacally detailed inspection of how twenty-three of "the thirty-nine framers of the original Constitution" voted during their careers on the issue of federal regulation of slavery. Lincoln had tabulated the results with all the dramatic flair of an insurance adjuster: his point is that the framers and signers, when in the Senate and the House, voted regularly both to extend and prohibit slavery, thereby giving at least a passive endorsement to the view that the Constitution allowed the federal government to legislate all its parts.

Yet the argument is carried on in numbing and what might seem to be irrelevant detail: after all, slavery wouldn't suddenly have become noble if the framers *had* reserved its governance for the states. Yet by making it plain that this *is* an argument, an appeal not to sentiment but to constitutional law, Lincoln places his own unqualified anti-slavery sentiment on the same drily legal and procedural grounds that he had recommended at the Lyceum. The result is the same, as he knew perfectly well. That's why the final cry of the Cooper Union speech is so suddenly uncompromising and even frankly warlike: "Let us have faith that right makes might, and in that faith, let us, to the end, dare to do our duty as we understand it."

Lincoln himself could not entirely abide by his own code. The discomfort he felt with the code of honor that surrounded him becomes plain in the story of the one duel he almost fought. Four years after the Lyceum speech Lincoln would actually be "called out" to fight a duel with James Shields, who had taken offense at an attack that Shields believed Lincoln had made on him in print (and that Mary Todd may have helped to sharpen). Although dueling was outlawed in Illinois, Lincoln answered the bell—so much for absolute obedience to law—and the duel was averted by common sense and conciliation only at the last moment. But as the British biographer Richard Carwardine says, Lincoln seems mostly to have felt embarrassed about its absurdity afterward and thought that it was one of the things that had cost him the Whig nomination for Congress in 1843. It is possible that, as Garry Wills has suggested, Lincoln deliberately set out to make the terms of the duel absurd, "letting nonsense work itself out to its own demise." Even his choice of weapon—he insisted on sabers— though it has at first a "martial," European ring, was probably shrewd and calculating: sabers gave the bigger Lincoln an edge in reach. But then he also said, with a dishonorable but lovable candor, "I didn't want the d——d fellow to kill me, which I think he would have done if we had selected pistols." Lincoln found the whole thing embarrassing. Mary Lincoln, after his death, wrote that an army officer visiting the White House had once asked her husband, "Is it true . . . that you once went out to fight a duel and all for the sake of the lady by your side?" Lincoln, according to Mary, replied, "I do not deny it, but if you desire my friendship, you will never mention it again." But—such was the power of the honor code—it also may be that the news of the duel was one of the things that made Mary Todd's father think that Lincoln might not be such a dishonorable choice as a husband for his daughter after all.

In the Lyceum speech there is still an amateur, apprentice quality to Lincoln's voice—there's a divide between the originality of what he has to say and the conventional fustian he says it in. As the years went by, he found new ways of speaking that had the same shapes as his thought, a new way of making closely reasoned legal argument ring with the sound of religious necessity—of making a case neatly put sound like a bell newly rung.

One rhetorical device, for instance, that he mastered was the drill of monosyllabic summation—the urge, natural to a lawyer, to say something hard one last time in short, flat words. In one way it's a variation of the high and low oscillations we find in Shakespeare: say it fancy first, and then say it plain right after. (Today we say it fancy in professional language, plain in popular books. That's our division of labor.) But where the usual rhetorical device is to take an abstract proposition and put it in concrete terms, Lincoln's habit was to restate an abstract proposition in language that might still be abstract but whose rhythmic simplicity makes it *feel* more concrete.

In his crucial "lost speech" of 1856, for instance, he countered the threat of Southern "disunion"—the blackmailing threat that if anti-slavery forces won, the South would just walk out of the Union, making things much worse—by insisting, radically, that this was not constitutionally possible. He addressed the argument, we're told in the surviving notes, to an (imaginary) Southerner in the audience and used fairly abstract language to make the case: "The Union must be preserved in the purity of its principles as well as in the integrity of its territorial parts." A tough but interesting proposition to follow: he means that the principle that the national government can make rules about things like slavery is as important as simply holding the country together in one formal union.

But then he finished by speaking to both North and South, saying with an almost comic clarity so intense that it was remembered after most of the rest was lost: "We will not go out, and *you shall not*" (emphasis in the original)—flat monosyllables summing up an argument not at all simple in its form. The argument was not made more particular; it was just made particularly plain. It was the same proposition put in a way that made its meaning impossible to escape. He said it once, and then he said it again, and the second time he said it, you couldn't miss the point of what he was saying.

Throughout his career as an orator, this habit—neat flat summary of an idea in plain speech after an elaborate windup in legal argument—was his own. It wasn't at all a commonplace of the time, which tended more toward rhetorical elaboration of the main point rather than reduction to its essence—the kind of big rhetorical climax that the young Lincoln himself had attempted, in a flat-footed way, in that 1838 speech.

You can find it, for instance, in his speech of June 26, 1857, in the Springfield State House, denouncing the *Dred Scott* decision. He takes on directly the ugliest of all the arguments that Stephen Douglas liked to use—that the real goal of the anti-slavery movement was intermarriage: "Judge Douglas evidently is basing his chief hope, upon the chances of being able to appropriate the benefit of this disgust to himself. If he can, by much drumming and repeating, fasten the odium of that idea upon his adversaries, he thinks he can struggle through the storm. . . . Now I protest against that counterfeit logic which concludes that, because I do not want a black woman for a *slave* I must necessarily want her for a *wife*. I need not have her for either. I can just leave her alone."

I can just leave her alone. The rhetorical mastery of that plain sentence, deliberately inserted after a lot of "fine" high phrasing ("fasten the odium of that idea upon his adversaries," "I protest against that counterfeit logic"), is potent both in its clarity and in its comic appeal to common sense. It's a punch line more than a catchphrase. And it gets from us the punch line's reward— laughter at a newly recognized truth: That's right! You don't have to sleep with the slaves after you free them; the "odious intermingling of the races" that they keep telling you will happen isn't inevitable at all! Why, you can just leave her alone!

And the same spell of simple summary was cast when Lincoln later took on Douglas's other nasty bit of racist cant, that "he was for the negro against the crocodile, but for the white man against the negro," with its clear implication that Negroes are to whites as beasts are to men. Lincoln said in a speech in Columbus, Ohio, in 1859: ". . . in a pre-eminent degree these popular sovereigns are at this work; blowing out the moral lights around us; teaching that the negro is no longer a man but a brute; that the Declaration has nothing to do with him; that he ranks with the crocodile and the reptile; that man, with body and soul, is a matter of dollars and cents." Once again the higher argument—about popular sovereignty and its meaning—is treated at length and then condensed into monosyllables that would still be startling today: the real proposition at stake is *that man, with body and soul, is a matter of dollars and cents.*

Some of his revisionist critics have tried to make Lincoln seem indifferent to slavery, or even a racist. The truth is that Lincoln's cause was the end of slavery; racism was a secondary problem, and though he was never as unequivocal about it as we might like, throughout his life he tried to make the fewest concessions he could to racism within the context of a society that was for the most part violently racist. As Max Weber says, the ethic of politics is responsibility, and its end is not to say things that sound good but that actually lead to real good; that is what divides political acts from pseudopolitical ones. In our time racism is the problem, and slavery an old nightmare never to be revived. In Lincoln's time, slavery was something far worse than a moral problem; it was a moral catastrophe, and racism merely the shadow that it cast.

Lincoln's basic take on slavery in America is that it should never have been allowed to happen, and the schemes for the colonization of liberated slaves back in Africa, which he gave up on very late, were ways of trying to pretend that it never had. But in his debates with Stephen Douglas, the openly and sometimes obscenely racist senator, though Lincoln often changed the subject he never surrendered the ground. He was a politician, trying to avoid unwinnable arguments and peripheral battles if it could help him advance on the central front—and the central front, from first to last, was the fight to end the growth of slavery and then to end slavery itself.

In the records of their debates in 1858 Douglas's racism still astounds. Mocking Lincoln's insistence that the Declaration of Independence included blacks, he says, "I do not regard the negro as my equal, and positively deny that he is any kin to me whatever." Those words marked not a fringe but a commonplace position. Lincoln's response is cautious and politic, and made for the crowd—the differences between the races will "in my judgment probably forever forbid their living together upon the footing of perfect equality"—but his point is clear, and radical in the circumstances: "Notwithstanding all this, there is no reason in the world why the negro is not entitled to all the natural rights enumerated in the Declaration of Independence, the right to life, liberty and the pursuit of happiness . . . in the right to eat the bread, without leave of anybody else, which his own hand earns, *he is my equal and the equal of Judge Douglas, and the equal of every living man.*" The emphasis is in the original record, as it must have risen emphatically from Lincoln's lips. (And the recorder, though he marked down that there was laughter at Douglas's scornful bigotry, marks down "Great applause" at the end of Lincoln's insistence.)

Though much later, during the war he would say honestly that he would free either no slaves, or all, if it would save the Union, this didn't mean that he was indifferent to the fate of slavery. He meant that if the South returned to the Union then slavery would once again be subject to the law—and this meant to the reality that the lawfully chosen president was one who had declared that the country could not survive half slave and half free, and that the purpose of the opponents of slavery was to "arrest the further spread of it, and place it where the public mind shall rest in the belief that it is in course of ultimate extinction."

John Jay Chapman, the great late-nineteenth-century American historian who wrote the life of the abolitionist William Lloyd Garrison, was not wrong to find in Lincoln many a half-tinted equivocation on the race issue, a touch too much grease for the intractability of the problem. Chapman believed that Americans never had, and never would, confront the true horror of slavery unsentimentally or recognize that the true heroes were the abolitionists who said a loud and simple No. (As late as the 1960s in Philadelphia, as I well remember, the Civil War was taught, even to classrooms half-filled with black kids, as a tragic war between two comprehensible causes, and the Abolitionists treated as dangerous fanatics.)

But slavery was the issue, and on that issue Lincoln didn't give ground. He gained it. In this case, the pop history has it right and the quavers and qualifications of professional history can at times mislead. The South did not secede in 1861 in a last-ditch attempt to save slavery and the concentration camp culture that went with it because of deep ingrown concerns to which the election of Abraham Lincoln was mostly a neutral or secondary side issue. It seceded in 1861 in a last-ditch attempt to save slavery and the concentration camp culture that went with it because Abraham Lincoln had just been elected president.

And, as the war went on, as John Stauffer has shown in his remarkable study of Lincoln's relations with Frederick Douglass, the much desired chimera of American popular history—the pol who grows in office—for once was achieved as a plain fact. As Stauffer shows, Lincoln at first avoided Douglass as a liability only later to receive him as a colleague and equal—"Here comes my friend!" was his greeting to Douglass when they saw each other in the reception after the second inaugural—and rose to the occasion of emancipation not just as an expedient, but as an exclamation. Lincoln's life was spent trying to end the enslavement of a people, and his life ended on that last sad bed because of what he was heard to say in favor of their enfranchisement—he spent his life trying to encircle their enslavement, and then to end it, and lived and died in that cause. For the majority of mankind, opposition to slavery, he had said, and he never wavered in this truth, "is not evanescent but eternal. It lies at the very foundation to their sense of justice."

The attempt to make Lincoln into just one more racist is part of the now common attempt to introduce a noxious equilibrium between minds and parties: liberals who struggle with their own prejudices are somehow equal in prejudice to those who never took the trouble to make the struggle. Imperfect effort at being just is no different than perfect indifference to it. Lincoln's equivocations on race are somehow equivalent to the outright racism of his opponents, then and later, as though the whole point is not that Lincoln was doing everything in his power to end the agony and assist the emancipation of an oppressed group, while those on the other side were doing everything in their power to prolong the agony and prevent the emancipation. A good man who plays footsie for an evening under the table with a single bad idea becomes the equal of a man who spends a lifetime sharing a slovenly bed with an evil ideology.

E ven in his most famous mature speeches, as president, the habit of flat summary still lurks and makes a unique kind of poetry. In his first inaugural, he includes a very heavy and hard-to-follow bit of legal reasoning:

> I can not be ignorant of the fact that many worthy, and patriotic citizens are desirous of having the national constitution amended. While I make no recommendation of amendments, I fully recognize the rightful authority of the people over the whole subject, to be exercised in either of the modes prescribed in the instrument itself; and I should, under existing circum-

stances, favor, rather than oppose, a fair opportunity
being afforded the people to act upon it—I will ven-
ture to add that, to me, the Convention mode seems
preferable, in that it allows amendments to originate
with the people themselves, instead of only permitting
them to take, or reject, propositions, originated by
others, not especially chosen for the purpose, and
which might not be precisely such, as they would wish
to either accept or refuse. I understand a proposed
amendment to the constitution—which amendment,
however, I have not seen, has passed Congress, to the
effect that the federal government, shall never interfere
with the domestic institutions of the States, including
that of persons held to service. To avoid misconstruc-
tion of what I have said, I depart from my purpose not
to speak of particular amendments, so far as to say that,
holding such a provision to now be implied Constitutional law, I have no objection to its being made express,
and irrevocable—

And only then he concludes with the famous, and far simpler,
"mystic chords of memory, streching [*sic*] from every battle-field,
and patriot grave, to every living heart and hearthstone, all over
this broad land, will yet swell the chorus of the Union, when
again touched, as surely they will be, by the better angels of our
nature."

He also used the device in that most brilliantly compressed of
all modern writing, the Gettysburg Address, where what is in fact
a complicated logical chain of reasoning gets turned into fifteen
one- and two-syllable words.

The argument of the address, made less mysterious than it
really is by its familiarity, is that a country dedicated to equality
has always been thought of as weak because it has seemed unlikely
to survive, since it would fall apart from within; in the middle of a

war to see what might happen, the soldiers in the war are willing to die in order to demonstrate that democracies are not in fact that feeble. The monument they offer is their own deaths. At the same time, the vindication of the Republic is also a vindication of the principle of liberty. There is in this, for all its brevity, a complicated back-and-forth between two arguments, one demonstrating the strength of democratic government to survive, the other insisting on the expanded frontiers of liberty for all men through the survival of democratic government. It is both an explicitly pro-Union and an implicitly anti-slavery speech.

Once again the case is summed up in mostly one- and two-syllable words: "government of the people, by the people, for the people, shall not perish from the earth." It is this habit of summation by simplicity that Lincoln puts in place of the normal rhetorical habits of his time, alliteration and eloquent periphrasis and all the other classical forms of elegant bloat. It is not *just* simple, and Lincoln, pursuing subtle points about law and liberty, very often isn't lucid in the usual sense of being transparent. What Lincoln masters is the condensation of complicated argument, a hard case put again in a simple way.

A love of the grease and a feel for the gist, the habit of compromise even at the cost of absolute clarity, a restatement of technical argument in emphatic simplicities, clarity achieved and helpful ambiguity sought—these were the heart of Lincoln's style, and of his soul. They explain why we still argue about him: he said very clear things against slavery—and, for a time at least, he was ready to keep the slaves if he could find a bargain to keep the South in the Union. Law is the practice of rules in a context of deals, and Lincoln believed in both.

There were other, higher-sounding ways to counter the Southern feudal–Walter Scott code. The now unfairly forgotten figure of Cassius Clay, of Lincoln's native state of Kentucky, comes to mind. Clay was as courageous an anti-slavery crusader as existed in the country, and one of the rare men of the South who grasped the scale of the danger and the threat to the Republic. But Clay's thought and language against slavery usually echoed the clarion call to a higher cause that was part of the cultural style of the South already. (It is one of the small ironies of American life that the boxer Muhammad Ali had a given name that spoke directly to the struggle for freedom in a way that his adopted name can only suggest.)

On a larger stage, the figure of John Brown was always there as a counter to Lincoln. Brown, too, made a crucial turn, toward radical abolitionism, and toward violence, in the late 1830s. The decade began with Nat Turner's slave revolt and its brutal suppression, and so it also marked the moment when the generally benevolent Jeffersonian view of slavery—an evil that would pass with time—became replaced in the South by various nascent forms of ideological racism: blacks were not an unlucky race not yet quite ready for emancipation but a subhuman one whose only hope for salvation lay in being kept in slave labor; the evil would never pass because it wasn't an evil.

As David S. Reynolds's superb biography has taught us, John Brown was as radical an abolitionist as existed, determined that slavery was not an unfortunate institution to be reformed but an absolute evil to be ended. Yet Brown differed from the mainstream of Northern abolitionism in his peculiar *affinity* for the South—both for the blacks he wanted to help liberate and for the slaveholders he wanted to destroy. Where William Lloyd Garrison, though utterly passionate and courageous in his denunciations, was a thorough man of the North, with lawyerly-journalistic gifts of argument and irony, Brown was a man of romantic feeling. Brown shared with the slave owners a romantic ideology of personal honor through violence. "Our white brethren cannot understand us unless we speak to them in their own language; they recognize only force," Brown's friend the black radical James McCune Smith wrote, using words that no Garrisonian abolitionist would have trusted but Brown grasped and admired. "They will never recognize our manhood until we knock them down a time or two; *they will then hug us as men and brethren*" (italics mine).

Brown set out, in effect, not to convert the South to Northern values but to convert the Northern abolitionists to the Southern code of honorable violence. He was a virus that was to prove deadly to the Old South because at some deep level he shared its DNA: its assumptions, its literature, and even some of its values—particularly the value of dying heroically for a cause rather than living honorably for one, and the companion value of forcing other people to die heroically for their cause, whether they quite wanted to or not.

Brown's acceptance of this feudal ethic forms the general background to his murderous night in Kansas on May 24, 1856. "We must show by actual work that there are two sides to this thing and that they can not go on with this impunity," Brown declared after watching his fellow abolitionists quake and tremble in the face of violent pro-slave mobs. He assembled a party of activists, including four of his sons and a son-in-law, armed them with swords, and marched them toward the little settlement of Pottawatomie Creek. Brown had his men bang on the doors of pro-slavery households, pretending to be lost travelers, in order to get the men outside. There he ordered them cut to pieces, watching impassively as his sons and other followers did the work.

Brown in Kansas at first might seem to be without any cue to action—he had been neither implicated nor particularly humiliated by the vigilantes—until one realizes that the real trigger was something that had happened two days before in Washington: a South Carolina congressman had beaten Senator Charles Sumner, of Massachusetts, nearly to death with the gold head of his cane for daring to speak out against the pro-slavery forces in Kansas and, in a feudal manner, for criticizing a kinsman of his. Sumner, though no pacifist, had been unable to defend himself. (His feet seem to have got caught under his little desk.)

This assault was put forward, instantly, as crowning proof of the difference between the Southern honor culture and the Northern procedural one: a Northerner could talk trash, but he couldn't make plays. Brown, one of his sons said, "went crazy—*crazy*. It seemed to be the finishing, decisive touch." It was not a cool evaluation of the potential uses of violence in Kansas but the transferred sense of humiliation that he felt on behalf of Sumner that drove Brown to the massacre.

Brown was never arrested or tried for the Kansas killings, and when he came back East, he found himself a hero, though not with the members of Garrison's abolitionist "establishment," who were firmly pacifist and consumed by their own sectarian squabbling. Instead, it was the high Transcendentalists, Thoreau and Emerson and Alcott first among them, who became Brown's fervent admirers and propagandists.

In a way it was an early instance of radical chic: the Transcendentalists preferred a real man to a squabbling set of Mrs. Jellybys. But there was more to it. They shared a disdain for materialistic Northern society, which Brown had bankrupted himself out of and the Transcendentalists viewed largely with baffled dismay. Whatever else Brown might have been, he was not a trivial man, or a worldly one: he was not a merchant with a Sunday cause. He was a free man already in a state of liberty.

He received the backing of a group of wealthy abolitionists who called themselves the Secret Six, though a less secret secret group is hard to imagine. They included Thomas Wentworth Higginson, the man who was later Emily Dickinson's patron. (There are traces of Brown's life in Dickinson's poetry, one essentially fanatic American imagination speaking to another.) From that time on, Brown was devoted to fund-raising and recruiting for his Southern-invasion plan, which soon centered on the federal arsenal at Harpers Ferry in what is now West Virginia. At last, on October 16, 1859, Brown, two of his sons, and eighteen colleagues, white and black, descended on Harpers Ferry and took hostage about thirty-five people who happened to be near the arsenal (and all of whom were treated with great consideration). They shot a couple of bystanders, including a free black and the generally well liked mayor of the town. But by the following night the arsenal had been surrounded by federal troops—led, with almost unbelievable serendipity, by Lieutenant Colonel Robert E. Lee, then of the U.S. Army, and his lieutenant, J.E.B. Stuart—and several of Brown's men had been killed, including his son Oliver. Brown still refused to surrender; the federals rushed the arsenal, and Brown was stabbed in the side and slashed around the head.

It was what happened immediately afterward that made Brown's reputation as a martyr and prophet. Transported to the arsenal guardhouse, Brown, bleeding from his head wound, calmly faced down his captors through the next twenty-four hours, arguing his case and, on the whole, shaming what remained of their moral conscience. With the insouciant openness that was until quite recently a feature of American life—Oswald, let's recall, gave a press conference on the night of the Kennedy assassination—dignitaries and reporters and even artists for publications, North and South, rushed in to interview him. The governor of Virginia, Henry A. Wise, sat in, as did Lee and Stuart.

Horribly wounded, expected to die, his son dead alongside him, Brown kept his cool and his words. He observed that he could have fled but hadn't, out of concern for his hostages ("I had thirty odd prisoners, whose wives and daughters were in tears for their safety, and I felt for them"). Pressed on the great question, he said simply, "I think, my friend, you are guilty of a great wrong to God and against humanity—I say it without wishing to be offensive—

and it would be perfectly right to interfere with you, so far as to free those you wickedly and willfully hold in bondage."When Jeb Stuart warned sententiously, "The wages of sin is death," Brown turned on him: "I would not have made such a remark to you if you had been a prisoner and wounded in my hands." And then he spoke plain truth: "You had better—all of you people of the South—prepare yourselves for a settlement of this question. You may dispose of me very easily—I am nearly disposed of now. But this question is still [to] be settled."

And they listened, recognizing the dignity and courage of the old man who was speaking. The really astonishing thing about Brown is the respect his mad act of terrorism earned from his enemies. Governor Wise went back to Richmond and called him "a bundle of the best nerves I ever saw, cut and thrust and bleeding and in bonds. He is a man of clear head, of courage, fortitude, and simple ingenuousness. He is cool, collected, and indomitable . . . fanatic, vain, and garrulous, but firm, truthful, and intelligent." Another pro-slavery politician called him "as brave and resolute a man as ever headed an insurrection," and said "in a good cause, and with a sufficient force, [he] would have been a consummate partisan commander." It was praise for a Southern gentleman, coming from others.

Brown triumphed rhetorically and, in the end, effectively at Harpers Ferry because the slaveholder's code of honor, though in many ways a scandal, was not entirely a sham. His enemies were not demons, though they served a cause in many ways demonic. They did not treat him as subhuman; they did not torture him to death instantly or lynch him, as they might well have done had he been black. They were impressed by his grasp of the code of honor, of his courage in combat and fearlessness in the face of death and one's enemies, and they honored him accordingly. Even his trial, though "fixed" at some level, was open and offered at least the formalities of fairness.

Mark Twain understood how this worked better than anyone. He never tired of attacking the Walter Scott–inspired honor cult of the South, and in the feud of the Grangerfords and the Shepherdsons in *Huckleberry Finn* he gave memorable form to its nihilistic absurdity. But he also understood the moral force that the code gave to individuals: in the same novel the moment when the solitary, aristocratic Colonel Sherburn faces down a lynch mob alone is, as Twain imagined it, a distinctly Southern scene. Even Garrison, a man of unexampled courage, could not face down a mob in Boston but had to be saved by the police. The honor code, pernicious as it was, was not entirely a fraud.

In one of the weirder and more cosmic ironies of the age, John Wilkes Booth, an idolater of the Southern code, was, as John Stauffer has written, "envious of Brown's martyrdom." "Lincoln," Booth later told his sister, "was walking in the footsteps of old John Brown but no more fit to stand with that rugged old hero— Great God! No! John Brown was a man inspired, the grandest character of the century." Honor and violence, even in the worst of causes, as Booth thought the anti-slavery cause to be, was better than Lincoln's "hidden craft" and legal cunning.

Yet all of this—the appeal to a natural code of honor rather than the procedural rule of law, the respect for violence as a test of personal integrity, the extreme value placed on acts of individual physical courage, the love of scaffold eloquence of a theatrical kind—was alien to Lincoln. Despite their shared hatred of slavery, he was in every way the anti–John Brown and John Brown in every way the anti-Lincoln. Lincoln thought, categorically, in moral terms, but his morality, as a lawyer's morality always should be, was translated into the terms of contracts and claims, accepted premises and fixed procedures, clear precedents and plain intentions. Compassion and common sense might alleviate the law, but the romance of violence and appeals to honor could never transcend it.

When Lincoln proposed a cult of the law, he meant it, and we miss the thread of continuity in his life if we miss the passion of his belief in dispassion. The law existed in order to remedy and cure old evils; the right way to cure this one of slavery, which was fixed in law, was by using the law to fix it. Seceding from the Union was seceding from the law—and law meant the possibility of change without violence. The South was wrong because slavery was wrong, but it was wrong, too, because you could not, in Lincoln's view, and as a matter of law, choose to secede at will from the Union. These two things were not separate for him. That slavery was wrong and that procedural democracy was the right way to fix it were two terms in the same equation seen at different times. Things get better by following the rules. Lincoln didn't think that due process and fair procedures were the ornaments of a just society but thought that they *were a* just society; if you did things in the right way, then things could be right.

Compared with the high words and just convictions of the Transcendentalist abolitionists, as Marx saw, these convictions were very weak tea, but that was the point. It takes a lot of effort to distill strong drink; anyone can brew weak tea—it just takes hot water and tea leaves. Strong drink is where we end the evening; weak tea is where we start the day. Moral exhortation was part of the special province of the moralist; the rule of law was part of the commonplace civilization of the country. The Constitution was backlit by the Declaration but front-lit by ordinary contract law; you couldn't cancel it because you didn't like the results. Once in, you were in and could no more back out at will when you didn't like the way things were going than a party to a contract could unilaterally back out because he didn't like the way the contract was affecting his bank account. What was at stake in the war was the survival of a liberal nation, and the test of its survival was whether it could enforce its own laws against a minority who didn't like them (the law that had one man rather than another elected president or, more locally, the law that said a fort belonged to the government that had built it). Legal reasoning and liberal thought were the same.

For Lincoln, the language of legal argument *was* the true language of liberal eloquence. It was high democratic thought in its plain form, the goddess in a postman's uniform. In Lincoln's mind and language, oaths and legal contracts, divine principles and working methods, all came together in one potent package. Usually, to say that Lincoln was legalistic implies that he was narrow; for Lincoln, law was the broad highway of reason and not the narrow snaking one of special pleading. It was not just an idea for him. The law was his home. It was the vine that he had climbed to comfort, the one sure ladder to safety in a land of lynch mobs. The point, always, was that law alone prevented violence and Hobbesian anarchy, a retreat to a tribal honor system and lynch mob rule that, on the frontier, was more than a notional possibility.

The irony, of course, which Lincoln could just glimpse then, was that his search for a purely reasonable approach, and a language that went with it, would unleash, and enable, organized violence of a kind, and on a scale, that had never been dreamed of before.

The year of his Lyceum speech, 1838, was a pivot year, a key year, the year when something distinctly Lincolnian—a radical faith in reason, cold in its demeanor but hot in its effect—began to emerge from the hard-running engine of ambition and canniness that would bring the poor bright boy who loved to read and write safe to a big house. In that year, Lincoln gave himself a hard task, to turn reason into a new kind of passion, legal argument into liberal eloquence. And it was as well a pivot year across the ocean, where another twenty-nine-year-old, born to a safe big house but with an engine of ambition that sputtered and stammered as much as it purred, would confront, at a similar moment of crisis, an oddly similar knot of problems.

CHAPTER TWO

DARWIN'S EYE

DARWIN'S DELAY · DARWIN IN 1838
UNITARIAN AND "RADICAL" PAST, CONVENTIONAL PRESENT
ALL FOR THE LOVE OF LOOKING
TWO CHEERS FOR NAIVE OBSERVATION
READING MALTHUS AND CONTEMPLATING MARRIAGE
GEMS OF THE 1838 NOTEBOOK
PHILOSOPHY MEETS THE FACTS · THE RETREAT INTO FAMILY
THE NATURAL PHILOSOPHY OF BABIES
A NEW KIND OF VICTORIAN FAMILY
ANNIE: HER GIFT, HER DEATH, HER MEMORIAL
PRESSURES AND PLEASURES OF A COMPACT TEXT
LEARNING FROM THE LOW:
DOGS AND PIGEONS AND THEIR BREEDERS
DARWIN THE NATURAL NOVELIST
GUESSES MADE TO LOOK LIKE LOOKING
SYMPATHETIC SUMMARIES; ANTICIPATED ATTACKS
ARGUMENTS FROM EYES AND LINKS
THE NEW VOCABULARY OF THE SLIGHT AND THE SMALL
WHAT IS "THIS VIEW OF LIFE"?
A STOIC'S VISION OF THE WORLD, A FATHER'S ELEGY FOR A CHILD

D arwin's delay is by now nearly as famous as Hamlet's and involves a similar cast of characters: a family ghost, an unhappy lover, and a lot of men digging up old bones. Although it ends with vindication and fame rather than slaughter and self-knowledge, it was resolved by language, too—by inner soliloquy forcing itself out into the world, except that in this case the inner voice had the certainties and the outer one the hesitations.

The delay set in between Darwin's first intimations of his great idea, the idea of evolution by natural selection, which first crystallized for him in 1838, and the publication of *On the Origin of Species* in 1859. By legend the two events were in the long run one: Darwin saw the adapted beaks of his many finches, brooded on what they meant, came up with a theory, sought evidence for it, and was prodded into print at last by an unwelcome letter from an obscure naturalist named Alfred Russel Wallace, who had managed to arrive at the same idea.

It seems to have been more complicated than that. One reason Darwin spent so long getting ready to write his masterpiece without getting it written was that he knew what it would mean for faith and life, and as Janet Browne's now-standard biography makes plain, he was frightened of being attacked by the powerful and the bigoted. Darwin was not a brave man—had the Inquisition been in place in Britain, he never would have published—but he wasn't a humble man or a cautious thinker, either.

But another reason seems to have haunted him. His own religious doubts were not rooted in his work. His scruples, like those of most thoughtful men of the time, had already been raised by the discoveries of geology, which had shown that the world was much older than had been thought; by the "higher criticism" of the Bible, which showed that the scriptures were much more inconsistent than one might like; and above all, by his sense that religion could not explain human suffering. For Darwin the problem of pain, and the fact of pebbles, was already more powerful than the possibility of previous evolution. Still, he sensed that his account would end any intellectually credible idea of divine creation, and he wanted to break belief without harming the believer, particularly his wife, Emma, whom he loved devotedly and with whom he had shared, before he sat down to write, a private tragedy that seemed tolerable to her only through faith. The problem he faced was also a rhetorical one: how to say something that had never been said before in a way that made it sound like something everybody had always known—how to make an idea potentially scary and subversive sound as sane and straightforward as he believed it to be.

He did it, and doing it was, in some part, a triumph of style. Darwin is the one indisputably great scientist whose scientific work is still read by amateurs. We still read the four essential Darwin volumes—*The Voyage of the H.M.S. "Beagle"* (1839), *On the Origin of Species* (1859), *The Descent of Man, and Selection in Relation to Sex* (1871), and *The Expression of the Emotions in Man and Animals* (1872)—to get a sense of what Darwinism is all about in a way that we cannot read, say, Newton or Galileo to understand physics. Of course, the theory of evolution by natural selection would have been true even if it had been scratched in Morse code on the head of a pin. But it would not then be Darwinism: a "view of life," in its author's words, not an ideology. (An ideology has axioms and algorithms; a view of life has approaches and approximations.)

Darwin was not a writer just by inclination; he was, uniquely among the great scientists, an author by trade. His books, even some of the most technical ones, were published by a commercial publisher, and he was subject to the same trials as other writers: editors who cut too much, royalty statements that showed too little. Darwin really was one of the great natural English prose stylists. He wasn't a poet in that vaguely humane sense of someone who has a nice way with an image; he was a man who had learned to cast his thesis in a succession of incidents so that action and argument became one. And as with all good writing, the traces of a lifetime's struggles for sense and sanity remain on the page.

Reading Darwin as a writer shows us a craftsman of enormous resource and a lot of quiet mischief. But it can also remind us that recent efforts to humanize him—to assure readers that the truth is not so hard to take, that Darwinism does not expel us into a void of cold chance—are unnecessary. The most humane and poetic side of Darwinism is already there because he put it there when he wrote it down.

By the spring of 1838, Charles Darwin was at the peak of the first wave of his public reputation. The greater wave would come in 1859, after the publication of *The Origin,* which turned a naturalist into a sage. This first, earlier one came after his return from his voyage round the world on the *Beagle,* and turned on the wealth of specimens he had brought back. Oddly, given what would happen later, Darwin at this moment was seen more as an intrepid explorer than as a man of ideas, a naturalist rather than a natural philosopher; the credit, and the awards, for analyzing and ordering his specimens all went elsewhere.

He didn't care. More than anything else in life, Charles Darwin liked to look at things. He liked to look at things the way an artist likes to draw, the way a composer likes to play the piano, the way a cook likes to chop onions: it is the simple root physical activity that makes the other, higher-order acts not just possible but pleasurable. We get a very partial and misleading image of Darwin if we think of him as the sage of the Mount, a Tennyson or Carlyle, one more nineteenth-century Nestor grappling with big ideas about life, mortality, and the generations, an image we can form if we scour his big books too much in search of big stuff. The true inner Darwin is most visible in the books that seem, to the modern reader, as much a puzzle, a self-denial, as Charles Dodgson's logic and math texts can seem compared with the *Alice* books. (And like Darwin's, Dodgson's dull books are the steel and sinew in his inspired ones; logic is to Dodgson/Carroll what looking is to Darwin.) Darwin shows himself as himself as much in dauntingly titled works, like *On the Formation of Vegetable Mould, through the Action of Worms* (1881, and actually a thrilling read if you like the heroism of worms—the comma in the title is perfectly placed) and *On the Various Contrivances by Which British and Foreign Orchids Are Fertilized by Insects* (1862), as he does in his four "great" books—he shows himself best by seeing others. He looks, as hard as he can, and sees processes, not just plants—his worms are actors, makers of vegetable mold and capable of primitive consciousness and, as we'll see, even a certain innate musicality— and this act of looking and organizing is for him the probity of intelligence.

Darwin was a conventional man from an unconventional family. His grandfathers, Erasmus Darwin and Josiah Wedgwood, were, as Jenny Uglow shows in her beautiful book *The Lunar Men,* close to the beating heart of the north of England's Enlightenment in its most progressive phase. In the reaction that overwhelmed the country after the French Revolution, their circles were persecuted, but the family tradition remained one of plain speech and freethinking. The idea of the evolution of life was one that Charles Darwin's own grandfather, Erasmus, had written a poem about just five years before his birth:

> *First forms minute, unseen by spheric glass,*
> *Move on the mud, or pierce the watery mass;*
> *These, as successive generations bloom,*
> *New powers acquire and larger limbs assume;*
> *Whence countless groups of vegetation spring,*
> *And breathing realms of fin and feet and wing.*

Yet Darwin also went to some lengths to make himself seem just another Victorian gentleman naturalist, ear pressed to the ground for the rumble of obedient earthworms. He lived in the country on an independent income, like Jane Austen gentry, surrounded by loyal servants and faithful gardeners. ("I have always felt it to be a curious fact," his son Francis wrote later, "that . . . the chief of the moderns, should have written and worked in so essentially a non-modern spirit and manner.") He was an extremely English Englishman, with an Englishman's desire never to sound like a know-it-all coupled with the Englishman's conviction that he alone knows it all. Yet, unusual for a man of "vision," he also always wanted to be liked. He wrote once to his son Willy that "you will surely find that the greatest pleasure in life is in being beloved; & this depends almost more on pleasant manners, than on being kind with grave & gruff manners. . . . Depend upon it, that the only way to acquire pleasant manners is to try to please *everybody* you come near, your school-fellows, servants & everyone."

This is odd advice to give even a Victorian child; not "to thine own self be true" but "be pleasing to all." Approval was always important to him. Writing to his close friend Joseph Dalton Hooker after receiving the Royal Medal for Natural Science in 1853, ostensibly for his laborious work on barnacles, he wrote, "I cared very little indeed for the announcement it [the official letter] contained. I then opened yours, & such is the effect of warmth, friendship, & kindness from one that is loved, that the very same fact, told as you told it, made me glow with pleasure till my very heart throbbed."

Darwin's desire to love and to be beloved, to please *everybody*—while of course, like all of us, getting his own way and pleasing only himself—is easy to trace to his childhood. He grew up in a loud, competitive family; the single fundamental reality of his childhood, after the death of his mother when he was eight, seems to have been his constant sense that he was alive only to disappoint his demanding, imposing doctor father. "You care for nothing but shooting, dogs, and rat-catching," his father said to him when he was a teenager, "and you will be a disgrace to yourself and all your family"—words that should be pinned as a reproachful reminder to the lapel of every father with a disorganized adolescent, not least because it was exactly in those activities, taken to a higher dimension, that the son would find himself and solve the mystery of species. Learning how dogs got bred and how rats tried to run away taught him more about how species change than formal education in the biology of the day could have.

If one word could sum up Lincoln's character, it would be *shrewd;* if one word, Darwin's, it would be *sensitive.* Lincoln grasped instantly people's capacities, their intentions, their weak points and their strengths. Darwin was a tentative judge of people, but he was acutely aware of their moods and emotions, and things that other people just passed right over hit him hard. Questions that seemed a little simpleminded to other people—what is morality? why do children laugh when they're tickled? what makes us blush, or shrug?—pressed on him to ask again why those things happened.

And always he loved to look. As a boy he was obsessed with beetles in a way that other boys are obsessed with marbles. He collected them, sought them out, leaped across small rivers onto rotting logs in search of them, and triumphed when he found a strange one. A famous story tells of how the young Charles was once so engrossed with collecting beetles that he put one in his mouth to leave his hands free to search for others. The beetle turned out to be of the kind that emits a strong acid in its own defense, which it did in young Charles's mouth. The boy hardly seems to have cared.

Yet—and this is what set him apart from most of the naturalists of his day, with their stamp-collector's *mentalité*—Darwin always *thought* as he saw; "I am a firm believer that without speculation there is no good and original observation," he wrote once. Darwin's turn of mind was encyclopedically visual, relentlessly explanatory—he asked a *why* question about everything he looked at, but his answer to every *why* question that he asked was to look again at exactly *what*. Intelligence comes in two kinds: the ability to break down a general proposition into specific instances and the ability to sum up specific instances in a general proposition—the analytic ability and the aphoristic gift. Men like John Maynard Keynes and Samuel Johnson had both; most of the rest of us are lucky to have a bit of just one. (G. K. Chesterton and George Bernard Shaw both had the supreme gift of summing up an argument in a phrase, but couldn't for the life of them see the practical consequences of an idea that sounded good when you said it—for example, what an honor-and-agriculture society would actually be like in modern times, or what the result of a planned economy run by a Superman would actually become.)

Darwin had both kinds of intelligence, but what makes him exceptional in intellectual history is that neither kind came in crisp, neat tones of conventional smartness. He could break things down, and he could build things up, but he couldn't do either one simply or neatly. This was surely the source of his father's frustration with him, and of his frustration with himself; it is exactly the trait that, most often, makes bright kids look dumb. Darwin was smart without being quick—he had no aphoristic intelligence, no ability to make a concise summary of a point. His intelligence worked at length, over time, and in the accumulation of incidents rather than in the incisive example. This was why even as an adult Darwin believed himself to be, despite the evidence of all his books, which are industry and accomplishment enough for any man, a slow or awkward writer. He wasn't, any more than George Eliot was; he was just a particular *kind* of writer, not a phrase maker or a caricaturist but an argument maker and a pointillist.

The great event of his professional life was the five-year voyage on the *Beagle;* it gave him the time to look and the space to draw out his understanding. Alongside the irascible Captain FitzRoy, for the first time in his life he wasn't under academic pressure, the pressure to be smart and prevail in a conventional setting, the kind of pressure that he had been under in medical school, where he had also failed ignominiously. He found himself on that trip, as all of us do at some point in life, and everything that happened afterward depended on the confidence that he'd won and on the realization that he'd had that the world is a strange, older, and more varied place than anyone had let on.

On his trip he looked at nature and read about rocks—he read the first volume of Charles Lyell's revolutionary book *Principles of Geology,* which explained that the earth is much more ancient than anyone had imagined and made Darwin think in terms of deep time as he looked at local formations. This double vision, short biological generations set against deep geologic aeons, was crucial to everything he would do afterward, and the fun of the *Beagle* voyage is that the juxtaposition was immediate, right there for the seeing, not bookish and learned.

Today, we read his account of that trip, *The Voyage of the "Beagle,"* searching for the occasional gestures toward an "evolutionary" view. We read it knowing what's coming, as we read the early Lincoln looking for signs and portents of what was to come for him. But what really knocks us out now is how much pure observation, pure plain looking, there is in Darwin's book. The poetry lies in the sweep of seeing. Over the course of several pages in *The Voyage of the "Beagle,"* we get an invocation of fireflies, an explanation of a leaping beetle, and an evocation of tropical sights:

> At these times the fireflies are seen flitting about from hedge to hedge. On a dark night the light can be seen at about two hundred paces distant. It is remarkable that in all the different kinds of glowworms, shin-

ing elaters, and various marine animals (such as the crustacea, medusæ, nereidæ, a coralline of the genus Clytia, and Pyrosma), which I have observed, the light has been of a well-marked green colour. . . . I found that this insect emitted the most brilliant flashes when irritated. . . . The flash was almost co-instantaneous in the two rings, but it was just perceptible first in the anterior one. . . .

I amused myself one day by observing the springing powers of this insect, which have not, as it appears to me, been properly described. The elater, when placed on its back and preparing to spring, moved its head and thorax backwards, so that the pectoral spine was drawn out, and rested on the edge of its sheath. The same backward movement being continued, the spine, by the full action of the muscles, was bent like a spring; and the insect at this moment rested on the extremity of its heads and wings-cases. The effort being suddenly relaxed, the head and thorax flew up, and in consequence, the base of the wing-cases struck the supporting surface with such force, that the insect by the reaction was jerked upwards to the height of one or two inches. . . .

During the day I was particularly struck with a remark of Humboldt's who often alludes to "the thin vapour which, without changing the transparency of the air, renders its tints more harmonious, and softens its effects." This is an appearance which I have never observed in the temperate zones. The atmosphere, seen through a short space of half or three-quarters of a mile, was perfectly lucid, but at a greater distance all colours were blended into a most beautiful haze, of a pale French grey, mingled with a little blue.

This is much harder to write than it seems; the range of reference, the precision of description—watch a bug jump and then try to put down exactly how he does it—weaving together references to Humboldt and tuning your fork to "a pale French grey." "The poet's eye, in a fine frenzy rolling, /" Shakespeare tells us, "Doth glance from heaven to earth, from earth to heaven; / And as imagination bodies forth / The forms of things unknown, the poet's pen / Turns them to shapes, and gives to aery nothing / A local habitation and a name." The naturalist's eye takes the same trip, only observation more than imagination occupies the seat, and gives to earthy somethings a local habitation, too, and, more than a name, a place in the whole.

It is normal now to mock slightly the writing of science as the sum of observation. For the past fifty or so years, philosophers of science and students of the scientific method have done all they can to end the idea that science is just accumulated observation, pure "induction" that leads eventually to a theory. The great philosopher of science Karl Popper, in a famous essay, pointed out that even the command "Observe!" is meaningless: observation demands a point of view, a problem, an issue. All seeing is impregnated with thinking. Physicists "observe" their particles only as we observe our athletes, in action in orchestrated moments. If science were simply a bucket into which descriptions fell, it would be a heap of facts. It is in the jump beyond, to a general rule, a theory, even a vision, that science advances. It is in the leap of the data, not the heap of the data, as Muhammad Ali might have put it, that the advance lies.

All of this is true, and a necessary corrective to an overly naive view of "inductive" science—the old idea, usually associated with the Elizabethan philosopher Francis Bacon, of science as unprejudiced observation rather than theory-laden thought. "Without speculation there is no good and original observation," as Darwin himself said. But as usual in life, the truth lies more often in the mushy middle than in the clear outline of the edge, and no one can do more than Darwin to remind us of the role of good old-fashioned observation in science—encyclopedic gathering together of close-order facts whose ultimate meaning, or even possible likeness, isn't clear to the observer when he makes them. The data has its music, too.

As one reads *The Voyage of the "Beagle,"* Darwin's Argus-eyed, relentless sheer *seeing*—his endless observations of spiders and vultures and snakes and beetles, of what it takes to check on the fatness of a tortoise or a lizard's method of swimming—is what is overwhelming. He seems to see everything, and as we accompany him, our eyes are opened, too. The discipline and practiced mindfulness that are necessary just to see all this—and in three "strata" too, in geology and botany as well as zoology, among the animals, plants, and stones as much as among the beasts and birds and bugs—are dearly bought. It seems transparent, and we think, "Oh, I could do that too." *That's* not where the greatness or genius resides. But it does, really.

Not long ago I found myself reading some of the "naturalist" sections of *Voyage of the "Beagle"* on a family holiday in the Caribbean, and I decided to test myself. I went out snorkeling one morning in the reef near the hotel, a well-breathed touristic reef of tropical fish, and struggled to keep track of all I saw—the many kinds of fish, and a few striking plants—and to recall how the fish behaved. Within ten minutes my mind was dazed by the effort. There is, first of all, the scrim of observer effect to get through: the fish are reacting to you as much as to their environment; you *are* the environment, for a moment. Even after you have paid the price of stillness for long enough to win some serenity, fish fly by, blindingly, and the twists and turns of schools and kinds—is that a zebra fish? is the other striped one the same sort, only smaller?—make you wince with effort. And then all the little inconveniences of nature—you practicing your breathing, keeping the view clean—interfere and affect your efforts at observation. After an hour I was scarcely able to squeeze out a coherent three sentences on what I had seen.

Imagine Darwin's tenacity and mental discipline, then, which show through in the seemingly artless pages of recorded nature in *The Voyage*. Nausea and heat stroke and hunger and exhaustion must have affected him time after time—there were very few untroubled or serene days on his voyage—and though some of the animals were "tame," far more were secretive. Yet he unspools page after page of pure observation that takes the breath away. The humble naturalist's task is, just from the sheer physical challenge, where all real mental work begins, harder than the cosmic poet's, or the natural philosopher's.

Could any of the other naturalists who had been considered for the job have done nearly as much, or as well? The discipline of observation *was* widespread in Darwin's visual culture. As much as Lincoln grew up in a rhetorical culture, Darwin, in a more closemouthed and less self-dramatizing country, grew up in a culture of close observation. He lived in a society of seeing, as Lincoln lived in a society of speaking. We are still startled to see how relentlessly the Victorians sketched and drew; Ruskin took it for granted that the educated class he was speaking to knew all about how to shade one side of a tree cast in sunlight. (Perhaps this is why the greatest portrait photographs of all are mostly Victorian; the camera was the ideal picture box for tongue-tied people with active eyes and a fear of showmanship; you could even hide your head.)

Yet Darwin is, with Ruskin, the greatest pure observer and describer of his time. He always strikes a note of first-person faux-naïf that is as winning as it is calculated. He can show faces and movement, and search for their meaning to a human correlate:

> This Trigonocephalus [snake] has, therefore, in some
> respects the structure of a viper, with the habits of a rat-
> tlesnake: the noise however being produced by a sim-

pler device. The expression of this snake's face was hideous and fierce; the pupil consisted of a vertical slit in a mottled and coppery iris; the jaws were broad at the base, and the nose terminated in a triangular projection. I do not think I ever saw anything more ugly, excepting, perhaps, some of the vampire bats. I imagine this repulsive aspect originates from the features being placed in positions, with respect to each other, somewhat proportional to those of the human face; and thus we obtain a scale of hideousness.

A scale of hideousness—keyed to human faces, things that resemble them can be judged sweet or evil.

He can capture locomotion: "The Tinochorus [rumicivorus] has a close affinity with quails. But as soon as the bird is seen flying, its whole appearance changes; the long pointed wings, so different from those in the gallinaceous order, the irregular manner of flight, and plaintive cry uttered at the moment of the rising, recall the idea of a snipe." Looking at the amateur Ruskin's sketches of Venetian architecture, we are similarly wowed by the filigree and surface rendering, the love for ornament and chase work.

It is certainly true that he did not have yet a fully developed theory until years later—Frank J. Sulloway has brilliantly disproved the idea that Darwin had seen his variety of finches on the islands and drawn his conclusions there. Yet intimations of his future beliefs exist, and suggest the subtlety with which Darwin addressed the subject before he was sure he could persuade the world, or even himself, that it was so. In an overlooked footnote Darwin hints, delicately, at what is becoming his view on the mutability of species. Commenting on how greatly different the species of plants and animals are on either side of the Andes, he blandly remarks that this difference shows that species have been created on either side of the mountains and adds, "The whole reasoning, of course, is founded on the assumption of the immutability of species; otherwise the difference in the species in the two regions might be considered as superinduced during a length of time." *Superinduced during a length of time* is evolution in an opaque phrase—deliberately boxed into a footnote and obscured by an odd word.

Superinduced is still so strange a word that, I notice as I type, the spell-checker on my word processing program does not recognize it. It was a very unusual word even in its time. A search through contemporary writing turns it up at last in John Stuart Mill, who uses it quoting Coleridge, whom Darwin, we know, read enthusiastically, and from whom he must have derived it. *Superinduced,* it turns out, is a fancy way of saying "added," with a special added note of "magically superimposed." Using the word was a clever way of very obscurely implying the possibility of mutable species without even vaguely committing to it as an empirical position.

Such hints aside, Darwin's themes, his point of view, *his* observational issues in *The Voyage,* are not evolution or competition but behavior and time, the eccentricity of nature, and the possibility of slow change (though not yet imagined to be under the pressure of adaptation or competition). He thinks that the natural world is weirder than you might expect it to be. Giant rats are there, hawks that are almost hawks—the world is a peculiar place, inhabited by colorful eccentrics. And there is, still, a certain "natural theology." "Among the scenes which are deeply impressed on my mind," he writes, "none exceed in sublimity the primeval forests undefaced by the hand of man; whether those of Brazil, where the powers of Life are predominant, or those of Tierra del Fuego, where Death and Decay prevail. Both are temples filled with the varied productions of the God of Nature:—no one can stand in these solitudes unmoved, and not feel that there is more in man than the mere breath of his body."

We tend to write and celebrate "revolutionary science"—great leaps of courageous imagination on the part of a handful of visionaries alter our understanding of the universe. But most science, including most of the science of The "Beagle," is "normal" science, small observations of established things that add to or alter in some small way what's already well understood. Yet how impressive it is, when viewed in the context of the ignorance and superstition that still raged and drove the scientist Joseph Priestly from his home in the north of England a generation before, to simply see the slow work of the naturalists, the fussy young and old men collecting beetles and watching butterflies. They are building a coral reef of small facts and observational detail, of study and scrutiny, that will protect knowledge of the larger kind, too. The harmless acts of observation built the coral of natural science, which became the jagged end of objectivity, a sharpened tool. The gentleman's hobby, the fusty naturalists with their notebooks, produced an incontrovertible mass of fact. Pettifogging observation made the antibodies that immunized theory against a fatuous dismissal. The birds differed; the bugs had adapted; the bones were there.

But Darwin was also capable, in a quiet way, of immensely ambitious theory making from a tiny load of empirical experience. He intuited, on his voyage, on a tiny summit of evidence, the history of, exactly, the coral reefs. The reefs were mystifying structures; they were made up of the carcasses of millions of tiny sea creatures that were known to live only in shallow water, and yet the accumulated coral spanned vast depths. How could that be accounted for? Darwin, just back from the Beagle in 1836, proposed that the islands were actually the tips of submerged volcanoes. He created the so-called subsidence theory: as volcanoes gradually sank, they offered their now just-visible summits as perfect tables on which coral could grow. A coral reef is just a funeral wreath around the tip of a defunct mountain.

It was a brilliant, simple, but immensely bold theory, and was immediately championed by Lyell himself, who helped sell it to the entire British geological establishment. It was Darwin's first intellectual triumph, and buoyed him through the long coming years when he worked on what became *The Origin*. It was also, as the historian David Dobbs points out, a Herschelian theory, after the Victorian astronomer and philosopher John Herschel, who pioneered the notion that science is a collection of stories about facts, not a mere collection of data dumps. Darwin's theory about subsidence jumped far beyond any data that lay at hand; Darwin had seen relatively few coral reefs, and of course neither he nor anyone else could ever have observed a volcano sink and a reef form around it. It was the first instance of the power of what would become typical Darwinian reasoning: what looks big, beautiful, and designed is just chance plus time—a volcano sinks, and tiny animals take advantage.

Like most Englishmen of his class and time, Darwin was a prisoner of respectabilities and of encircling embarrassments. Home from the voyage, safe within his own city house and garden, though, he was far from diffident or unsure. The tone of his notebooks, as of his private letters, became ironic, impatient, quick-tempered, and he rushed to confident speculations on the basis of small evidence.

Few documents are more fun to read than his notebooks of the late 1830s, where his ideas about evolution are already alive and you see his mind at work, unafraid. They are among the golden books of science, as much fun to read as a notebook of sketches. They were composed in what he later called "a mental riot," where, as he said at the time, he chose "to let conjecture run wild."

He thinks wild thoughts—that there's nothing so remarkable about man, with all his brainpower, appearing on earth; the amazing thing is that mind appeared at all. Man's rise is "nothing compared to [that of] the first thinking being." He follows strange lines of thought: what if animals are as worthy of humane treatment as the slaves he had seen treated so cruelly on his voyage? After all, all living things "may partake from our origin in one common ancestor; we may be all netted together." *Netted together*—drawn together not in one neat hierarchical chain of being but entrapped in one common web of life. The ladder of life is replaced in a phrase with the growing bush of organisms. "Plato," he writes, "says in Phaedo that our 'necessary ideas' arise from the preexistence of the soul, are not derivable from experience.—read monkeys for preexistence." *Read monkeys for preexistence.* Metaphysics is instantly collapsed into biology.

Darwin's notebooks of 1838 mark the real beginnings of his evolutionary thought and are a monument in the history of the modern mind—but they are among the most charming and ingenuous monuments ever made, a coral reef of many small free speculations that has since turned into bedrock. The more purely observational Darwin of the *Beagle* is gone, and his mind now races from poetry to psychology to philosophy and back again. The line between the empirical and the philosophical—for that matter between the scientific and the literary—is broken, "disrespected" as kids say today, in a way that makes something genuinely new to thought. Philosophical concepts are tested by natural facts, and natural facts are always searched for what they mean about man and history.

This process is obviously part of what every natural philosopher might do—but few before the young Darwin are quite as stunningly specific in their natural facts, or as searchingly unorthodox in their philosophies. Darwin sweeps through poetry and observation, seeking in *The Faerie Queene* for evidence about the origins of expressions, and in Burke's essay on the Sublime and Beautiful for truth on the question of why people cry. The young Darwin is unafraid of blunt speculation: "Blushing is intimately concerned with thinking of ones appearance—does the thought drive blood to surface exposed, face of man, face, / upper / bosom in women: like erection . . ." He goes to the keeper for information about the sexual behavior of monkeys in the newly chartered London zoo: "A very green monkey (from Senegal he thinks Callitrix Sebe??) he has seen place its head downwards to look up women's petticoats." He struggles to place philosophy on a natural footing: "Origin of man now proved.— Metaphysics must flourish.—He who understand baboon would do more toward metaphysics than Locke." His mind is testing, probing, reading, and taking in evidence equally from the classics and from his own observation.

At the core is a new practice—the old philosophical ideas of aesthetics and attraction, of what sexual allure is and what makes beautiful things look beautiful to us, can be tested not by more philosophy but by actual evidence from observation. And behind the new practice looms a new idea, his "theory"—that mankind is not a shining poem apart but one page in the long history of life, which blends seamlessly from one era to another and one species to another, and where when man wiggles his ears he is recalling his primeval past: *He who understand baboon would do more toward metaphysics than Locke.*

The flights of philosophy to observation and back are rapid and winning. He takes a passage in which Hume argues that some ideas *become* unconscious to mean that some ideas "order muscles to do the action," make instinctive grimaces that men share with animals. But then he tests the abstract idea against his experience of monkeys: "Another little old American monkey / Mycelis / I gave nut, but held it between fingers, the peevish expression was most curious. remember the expostulatory angry look of black spider monkey when touched. . . . The ourang outang, under same circumstances, threw itself down on its back & kicked &

cryed like naughty child.—do monkeys cry?—(They *whine* like children.)" And then he draws what will remain his conclusion: "Expression is an hereditary habitual movement consequent on some action, which the progenitor did when excited or disturbed by the same cause, which, now, excites the expression." Babies sneer to show the canine teeth, though those teeth no longer really threaten, because our ancestral animals made their threats in that way, too.

There are, as Howard E. Gruber in his commentary on the notebooks has written, only occasional gestures toward adaptation; Darwin hasn't settled on its importance, yet. But he is already a materialist and aware of the extent of his materialism. "Mine is a bold theory," he admits at one moment, but it is not a crude one: matter, the ancestral past, shapes our minds and our appetites; our minds make ideas, and the ideas change matter. He sees that the constant human need for causation makes "savages" think that a god must cause thunder and lightning. But what really interests him is that the inborn urge toward explanation makes it happen, that even science begins in the basic struggle to understand, the theory-making propensity common to all living things: "All science is reason acting/systematizing/on principles, which even animals practically know (art precedes science—art is experience & observation)." (Art is "experience & observation" in the sense, one gathers, that it can record behavior without supplying explanation—we don't need to know what *causes* Hamlet to find him interesting.)

He mocks man's arrogance. In one of the "transmutation" notebooks he writes: "If all men were dead then monkeys make men.—Men make angels." (That is, the monkeys would seem the most astounding of all creatures, set apart from the rest of creation, while creatures with gifts like man's would be seen as supernatural.) But he doesn't deny men's agency, or our minds. There is a lovely, telling small note where, just after his reflections on monkey expressions, he writes: "Nothing shows how little happiness depends on the senses [more] than the [small] fact that no one, looking back to his life, would say how many good dinners . . . he had had; he would say how many happy days he had spent in such a place." We have sensual experience, animal appetites, and arrive at the idea of happiness. Happiness is made of many dinners, but the dinner provokes a concept larger than just their enumeration. Sensation becomes conceptual thought. The mind turns good dinners into happy days.

It was in 1838, amid this quiet riot of thought, that Darwin had the two experiences that locked him in place for the next two decades. On the one hand, he read Thomas Malthus on population, and "got a theory," or a guide to it; on the other, he decided to get married, to his cousin Emma, which would lead, for a time, away from theory altogether.

"Poor Malthus!" Sydney Smith had written almost four years before, on the occasion of the clergyman's death. "Everybody regrets him;—in science and in conduct equally a philosopher, one of the most practically wise men I ever met, shamefully mistaken and unjustly calumniated." Malthus's "Essay on the Principle of Population," in which he is thought to argue—whether this is actually the argument he intended to make is still debated, or whether he was actually "shamefully mistaken," horrifically misunderstood—that as population grows geometrically while food production can increase only arithmetically, starvation is the only cure for overpopulation. (Compare Scrooge in *A Christmas Carol:* "If they would rather die, they had better do it, and decrease the surplus population.")

Darwin, in his *Autobiography,* tells us that

> in October 1838, that is, fifteen months after I had
> begun my systematic enquiry, I happened to read for
> amusement Malthus on *Population,* and being well pre-

pared to appreciate the struggle for existence which everywhere goes on from long-continued observation of the habits of animals and plants, it at once struck me that under these circumstances favourable variations would tend to be preserved, and unfavourable ones to be destroyed. The result of this would be the formation of new species. Here, then, I had at last got a theory by which to work.

Reading, like seeing, is selective, and in Malthus he found not a model but a mechanism. What drew Darwin to Malthus was not an encompassing vision of a planet of competition but the specific point that organisms make more children than their environment can support, and that the ones that survive must survive for a reason—might be ones that have some feature that gives them an advantage. A baby bug that could see farther than its brothers might get to the crucial crumb of bread first. (Malthus's argument eventually foundered on an error: population increases geometrically while food stocks can increase only arithmetically, he insisted. Fortunately, at least so far, that hasn't been true.)

There are ongoing arguments about just how much of Malthus there is in Darwin, and how much of Darwin is anticipated in Malthus. Malthus can have an unpleasantly sanctimonious tone, unknown to his student, and the moralizing is quite overt. (A shaming but perhaps not unique confession: until becoming preoccupied with Darwin, I had always thought that Malthus was a grim seventeenth-century figure, like Hobbes.)

Yet we are also undergoing a bit of a Malthus renaissance now, as ecology-minded "realists" insist that the central insights of Malthus about populations and resources are, like them or not, "neutral" and that the time of plenty through which we have just passed will prove to be a bubble on a Malthusian sea of pain. Darwin understood early on that where people were concerned,

Malthusian argument was really not about nature but about culture, where purposes count—about how we are prepared to share resources. We share not against nature but because, as social animals, it is in our interest to help one another. Scrooge's moral education is to learn that Malthus is right only if we let him be. (Darwin would later come to reject the Malthusian idea that poverty could be cured only by famine.) Darwin learned from Malthus, as Marx learned from Darwin, but he wasn't a Malthusian. The theory Darwin got worked only where no conscious intentions were working at the same time.

Yet Darwin did understand clearly, and began to brood at length on, what he eventually called the "wedge" of death, the reality that his new theory implied that death and suffering and pain were, from some point of view, creative but not justified. It wasn't that suffering was for your own good, or for the good of the species; suffering just *was*. It might in the long run produce innovation, but that wasn't its point. Its point was—well, its point was a dagger pointed at the heart of "natural theology," which insisted that nature, though cruel seeming in individual cases, was purposefully benevolent seen whole. The infliction of suffering in that view implied not a long-term direction but a perfected balance, a plan; we suffer for a purpose. This kind of Panglossian hopefulness Darwin dismissed. "Pain & disease in world, & yet talk of perfection," he wrote in his notes. Even if civilized people could temper the Malthusian horror for man, nothing could alter it in the long course of nature. Death was the thing that weeded out life. The process might have a history, but it didn't seem to have a moral or, really, a point.

Perhaps in spite of this new preoccupation—or, perhaps, in order to spite it—he began to think about getting married. He made a series of reflections on the advantage of marriage that is irresistibly comic, charming, because it attempts to use the same kind of close-order analytic reasoning on the question of whether to make love to a woman as led to his revelations on coral reefs. In a famous series of notes, he made a "pro" and "con" list of the advantages and drawbacks of getting married, like Robinson Crusoe on his island pointing out the positives and negatives of being shipwrecked. (Did he have a particular bride in mind? It isn't entirely clear.)

Against, he listed: "Freedom to go where one liked—choice of Society & *little of it.*—Conversation of clever men at clubs—Not forced to visit relatives, & to bend in every trifle.—to have the expense & anxiety of children. . . . I never should know French,—or see the Continent—or go to America," or even "go up in a Balloon." For the idea, he noted: "Children . . . —Constant companion, (& friend in old age)" and, memorably, "better than a dog anyhow." In the end, he chose marriage, on the strong grounds of "a nice soft wife on a sofa with good fire, & books & music perhaps." "Marry—Marry—Marry Q.E.D.," he concluded.

There is so much inadvertent poetry on this page that as it brings a smile to one's lips, it is perhaps easy to miss the slightly tongue-in-cheek quality it must have originally had for its author. Common sense tells you that Darwin was not a kid, nor a naïf, and he had seen enough of the world in five years' circumnavigating it to know something of sex and men and women. He is having fun, as he always does in his notebooks, fooling around with an idea in a deliberately po-faced manner that was part of his humor. It is fair to guess, given the intensity of his obsessive interests already, that the idea that marriage would keep him from going up in a balloon was not actually a real concern. (On the other hand, the notion of America might have been; he would toy with the idea of emigration even after he was settled and housebound.) The combination of earnest naïveté in the attempt to project the future and a gauche and winning boyishness—only a newcomer to it would have counted the conversation of clever men in clubs enough to swear him to a celibate life. (It is also very much like Darwin that he did not put the expected exclamation point at the end of the that triple "Marry.")

The woman he was to propose to, his cousin Emma Wedgwood, had a bit more Jane Austen in her than might first seem apparent. Pretty in that sleepy early-Victorian manner, she had a sharper tongue, on paper at least, than her reputation as a pious, retiring mama might suggest. Just that year she had written in a letter about her disappointment with a life of Bishop Wilberforce that she was reading: "His dull sons have put in such a quantity of repetition that one is quite weary of the same religious sentiment repeated 50 times over in nearly the same words. And they have been very spiteful about poor old Clarkson, who is blind and 80 years old, which I think might have made them careful not to hurt him, and one feels very sure their father never would. Wilberforce's letters, I think, are not very agreeable or clever, but very sweet (in a good sense)." She bantered with the best, writing to Darwin, after they were engaged, "You will be [after our marriage] forming theories about me & if I am cross or out of temper you will only consider 'What does that prove'. Which will be a very grand & philosophical way of considering it."

But that she was passionately religious, a woman of faith, there's no doubt. They exchanged letters on the great questions. It seems clear that Charles confided in her his hopes: his belief that he had stumbled on a fundamental discovery about life's history, and that he was on the way to solving the "mystery of mysteries." In stating his hopes, he could not help but confess his doubts. It was, as he would say elsewhere, like confessing a murder. And she seems to have said to him unequivocally that it would pain her beyond measure if indeed he believed these things and went ahead and said them publicly. Her reasons were sympathetic and even romantic: they would not be able to stay together through eternity. "My reason tells me that honest & conscientious doubts cannot be a sin, but I feel it would be a painful void between us."

Whether Charles promised to stay away from his speculations, or promised himself to, or, most likely, decided to throw himself into more conventional kinds of naturalism while saving the bigger thoughts for another day, he certainly drew back from his revelation in the very moment that he had come close to the truth. He turned instead to the detailed study of the kinds and habits of—barnacles. He had good reasons to delay: he wanted the argument to be impregnable; he wanted to be an unimpeachably big deal naturalist when he published. "Darwin? Well, you know, his stuff on barnacles *is* very sound." "No one has hardly a right to examine the question of species who has not minutely described many," he wrote to his friend J. D. Hooker in 1845, and one hears Darwin trying to convince himself that the drudge work must precede the real work. (This intuition was sound, though, at the tactical level; he eventually got that Royal Medal "All along of the Barnacles!!!" as Hooker wrote to him delightedly.) He needed much more time to get the details right and the problems solved. But there was also, undeniably, an element of fear and hypersensitivity in his delay—fear of the critics, of course, but also fear of hurting the one person he loved most by saying things that would pain her.

But he knew he was right, and he knew it already. He was torn. He did eventually write a précis of the theory, complete, in 1844, and wrote a letter to Emma enjoining her to publish it if he died suddenly. In it, he pointed out what remained the central challenge to his theory—the argument from the design of the human eye, which seems too perfectly wrought to have emerged by small natural steps rather than one big creative act. He sketched his idea of what we now know to be the right solution: that the eye is neither perfectly designed nor all that hard to make by slight increments, since half an eye is much better than no eye at all. But Emma wrote in the margin, referring to the idea that a mere light-sensitive nerve could become a perfect seeing machine, "a great assumption, E.D."

He respected his wife enough to listen to her opinion and knew, as well, that her opinion was likely to be the opinion of the world, whose reflexive attitudes, on this subject at least, she knew by heart, and by soul, too. Whether he promised her to go no further, for a while anyway, or promised himself to publish nothing until he was certain, he knew that he was right and that he couldn't say what he knew, not yet. He was in something like the position of an addict who promises to leave the needle or bottle alone but, deep inside, knows he can't. The notebooks from the late 1830s were always there, somewhere on a high shelf in his mind. A deep ambivalence was set in Darwin's character beginning in 1838. He *was* working hard, accumulating evidence, refining his theory—but he was also getting deeper into barnacles, finding ways of avoiding the point, finding excuses for not finishing or publishing.

Sex and family and earthworms and barnacles more than made up for it. Despite Peter Gay's long urging us to accept the existence of intense erotic life between married people in the Victorian era, we still tend to have an oddly prim view of the sex lives of our great-great-grandfathers. Emma and Charles had ten children in seventeen years—but we nonetheless act as though these constant pregnancies and "confinements" are not the sign of a lovemaking so urgent and regular that it could defy chance to produce so many full-term pregnancies. A woman is not always pregnant if a man is not always asking. What Darwin did have was a puzzling opacity about the reasons his wife was always pregnant, as Dickens, his contemporary, had about *his* wife's pregnancies. More than any other feature, this is strange—not "prudery" about sex but the need for it and the participation in it, along with a reluctance on the part of the man to take responsibility for its consequences. One can only believe that the Darwins enjoyed a good sex life, and that the dependency they show on each other, which shines through their letters and memoirs, was a function of it. Marriages are made of lust, laughter, and loyalty, and though the degree of the compound alters over time, none can survive without a bit of each one. We can usually infer the presence of all three from the presence of one; people are loyal to each other because of remembered pleasures, and they remember social pleasures because they recall sexual ones. All good marriages are different, but they are all alike in having the three elements in some kind of functioning, self-regulating balance.

That the Darwins felt lust is evident in their children; that they shared it is evident in their laughter. And that they laughed a good deal is obvious from their letters. They joke fondly—single-mindedly—about their children, because that's what parents do. But they had made this life together. It is always hard to resist projecting backward to an earlier time the values of our own time, particularly when those values are dear to us. We want the Darwins (like the Lincolns) to be loving and indulgent and attentive parents because then they will be like us. We should resist too facile a likeness. Charles Dickens, though family celebrating (he called his journal *Household Words* until his separation from his wife, when it became *All the Year Round*) and capable of writing fondly about his children (who called him Old Wenables), was obviously a remote and overbearing patriarch who scared his children, particularly the boys, half to death.

But with the Darwins the evidence is overwhelming and disarming that they were pioneers of engaged parenting. Charles, in fact, was so enraptured by the experience of having children that he made among the first stabs on record at true developmental psychology, the scientific study of children—what he called, beautifully, the "Natural History of Babies," a subject that no one would return to with such objective passion until our own time. (I know a famous developmental psychologist, a fanatic evangelist for the mental powers of the small, who insists that Darwin made a wrong turn by not pushing forward with his work on child psychology, rather than taking the more obvious turn toward what are, after all, mere footnotes in antiquarian biology. Kids' minds are primary; old bones are secondary.)

He made extensive notes on it. His love for his children, and his engagement with them, is genuinely startling for any time, and almost incredible in his own. "However hard my father was at work," his son George remembered years later, "we certainly never restrained ourselves in our romps about the house, & I sh^d certainly have thought that the howls and screams must have been a great annoyance; but we were never stopped." Charles studied his sons as though each were a barnacle, or a South American beetle: "W. Erasmus. Darwin born. Dec. 27th. 1839.—During first week, yawned, stretched himself just like old person—chiefly upper extremities . . . Surface of warm hand placed to face, seemed immediately to give wish of sucking, either instinctive or associated knowledge of warm smooth surface of bosom." *Either instinctive or associated knowledge*—the question of what's inborn and what's learned begins right after birth. He did not mechanize his children; he recognized that they were creatures of mind: he saw them unfolding jealousy, self-recognition, then recognizing that other people had minds like their own. He saw the moment when Willy learned that a mirror image was only an image and became "aware that the image of person behind, was not real, & . . . turned round to look at the person behind." Unsure whether the pleasure baby Willy showed in music was real or a figment of his parents' observation, he noted that Willy "cried, when Emma left off playing the pianoforte." The baby showed such "decided pleasure" as soon as she turned around to go back to the piano that Charles was certain the love for music was actual.

Of course, at one level, all of these things were things that mothers had known for millennia. (Emma didn't have the time to make notes at that length. Those of hers that survive are just as good.) You didn't have to tell mothers that babies love music any more than you had to tell milkmaids that cowpox ward off small-pox, or small boys dozing in a classroom that the continents fit together too neatly, jigsaw-puzzle-style, to not have once been one, or, as we'll see, than you had to tell pigeon fanciers that they could turn a pigeon into any kind of pigeon they liked. A large part of every scientific discovery, Darwin's included, involves paying attention to the long ignored.

What was new was that a father, a patriarch, was there to set them down. We insist, sometimes pugnaciously, that fathers have been remote in all times but our own, but this is a belief only of the Grumpy Old Guy school of family history, and may have been a singularity of American parenting circa 1938, perhaps because of the Depression. It was certainly not Darwin's view, or experience. The notes on the natural history of babies, more than anything else, show that he was there, in the nursery, and then with the children almost all the time: "I was playing with Baby," he writes to Emma in 1845, when she is briefly away from Down House, the country house they had made their home, "in the window of the drawing-room this morning and she was blowing a feeble fly and blew it on its back, when it kicked so hard that to my great amusement Baby grew red in the face, looked frightened, and pushed away from the window. The children are growing so quite out of all rule in the drawing-room, jumping on everything and butting like young bulls at every chair and sofa."

Probably the release into a tribe of children, butting like bulls, whom he could kiss and fondle and tease, was a huge liberation for a man brought up in a competitive and loving but far from fond family. And probably, too, we underestimate the amount of sheer joie de vivre that was possible in those locked-up houses. Samuel Butler, with his tight-lipped and closed-hearted Victorians in *The Way of All Flesh,* should not be our only guide; the wonderful Molly Hughes, writing of a slightly later date and a much poorer family, gives witness to the same kind of domestic pleasure but with absolute wild commitment to play. Sex and play were available to Victorian people as much as they are to us; the Victorians just talked about them less.

That both Darwin and Lincoln held their public life in tension with this obsessive inward-turning domesticity is hardly surprising—it is one of the key passions of their time. Victoria and Albert are the prime examples of the phenomenon, surrendering the louche, worldly manners of the aristocracy to which they belonged for the prim domesticity of the bourgeois family. But what is easy to miss is how much of it was rooted in awakened sexual love—as was certainly the case with Victoria's infatuation with her handsome Albert—and how much of it was happy. Lytton Strachey saw a great deal about the Victorians. He saw their hypocrisies, and we have recently been reinstructed in their virtues; what is most appealing about them, as the Darwins remind us, are their pleasures. Darwin's daughter Henrietta (whom everyone called Etty) writes—and there is no reason to think that memory cast more than the appropriate amount of gold varnish on her image—that high summer at the Darwin home meant "the rattle of the fly-wheel of the well, drawing water for the garden; the lawn burnt brown, the garden a blaze of colour, the six oblong beds in front of the drawing-room windows, . . . the row of lime-trees humming with bees, my father lying on the grass under them; the children playing about, with probably a kitten and a dog, and my mother dressed in lilac muslin, wondering why the blackcaps did not here sing the same song as they did at Maer."

And it came at a familiar social cost: the inward-turning bourgeois family is, from a dour view of the puritanical historian, a bit of the Hummer of human arrangements, a gas-guzzler of social capital. All the social goods are drawn inward while less fortunate classes are put to work to sustain the privileged unit—the Darwins had a staff of about a dozen, whom they patronized—while offstage Chartists roar and the working classes struggle for identity (and for the vote) and the tranquil daydream of garden and nursery goes on.

But, as Tocqueville and Voltaire alike have taught us, the man who cultivates his garden is likelier to be the man who worries about other people's ills than the man who has to scramble for roots or the one who scribbles in his study. Court practices and city values, of the kind Darwin had absorbed in London, bend toward a hypersensitivity to status—status in the academy, or in the university—while garden life bends toward family practices and family values, with their hypersensitivity to security. The bourgeois obsession with security has its ugly side, but it also has a blessed one. As Tocqueville had seen a little while before, home-making, which ought to make people more selfish, often makes them less so; it gives them a stake in other people's houses. It is not so much the establishment of a garden but the ownership of a gate that moves people from liking a society based on favors to liking one based on rights. Enclosing our garden broadens our circle of compassion.

Certainly, it did for Darwin. Though remaining very much what he was born to be, a wealthy landowner struggling with the realities of post–free trade Britain—"although I am on principle a free-trader, of course I am not willing to make a larger reduction than necessary to retain a good tenant," he wrote once, waspishly, to his agent—he also became acutely conscious of injustice and cruelty, and impressed his children with his energy against the exploitation of child labor, and against local cruelty to animals.

Of all those children, his favorite was his second child and first daughter, Annie. Her particular appeal to him is hard to name, but it's obvious from the earliest letters that he wrote about her. Darwin, like any father, loved all his children equally, and had his favorites, too. One has the strong sense that he saw himself in Annie—a slight awkwardness, a desire to please people, a sensitivity, and above all, an urge to learn. In one way, she seems to have been the Beth March of the Darwin family, the girl all loved. But she wasn't shy or retiring, just the opposite, really. For any parent, the possession of a child who seems to reproduce one's own characteristics is special, and a child with real curiosity must have seemed like the chief blessing in the life of a curious man. "Father, I have a question"—those words, natural to any bright child, seem to have fallen from Annie's lips more often than from her brothers'.

No, it wasn't her Beth March qualities that her father loved, her angel-in-the-house femininity. It was her intelligence. We know that she had the habit, unusual in anyone and unencouraged in most Victorian girls, of reading dictionaries, searching for the meaning of words. One imagines her loving if slightly baffled mother braiding her hair as the sensitive and serious girl reads; one feels that she fell on the Darwin rather than the Wedgwood side of this very inbred family. There's no stronger or more confounding emotion in the world—one that brings the mystery of reproduction and sex more brightly to a sensitive man's attention—than the existence of a child of the opposite sex who resembles *you,* no bigger emotion than the love that a father feels for a girl child in whom he nonetheless sees not her mother but himself.

Darwin's immersion in his family life—the Darwin family would later play bassoons to earthworms, to see if the worms could hear—also nearly came at a scientific cost. Although Darwin was working throughout, you can't escape the feeling that his reluctance to publish, his delay, was partly a reluctance to give up the serenity of the life he had found for the anxiety of the intellectual battlefield, which, he knew—or thought he knew—awaited him at the other end of publication.

Darwin's illness, of course, intruded as well. By now, there are as many diagnoses for Darwin's puzzling recurrent sickness as there are occasions of it. They run from the purely psychosomatic—Darwin was sick with self-doubt—to the entirely medical—Darwin had contracted Chagas' disease on the *Beagle.* In his letters, his illness certainly sounds more physical—episodic and baffling—than psychological. (Psychological ailments are usually pervasive and depressing.) Yet though clearly the sickness was "real"—Darwin had to have Emma write letters for him to correspondents when he was too ill to write himself—when he's up and writing his letters, he sure doesn't *sound* like a sick guy. On the contrary, throughout the 1840s, his letters ring with the sound of a happy man at happy work, a man in love with his work and wife and children. Writing to Emma in 1848, when he is away tending to his sick father, he writes, "Thanks for your very nice letter received this morning, with all the news about the dear children: I suppose now & be hanged to you, you will allow Annie is something. I believe, as Sir J.[ohn W.] L[ubbock] said of his friend, that she is a second Mozart, any how she is more than a Mozart, considering her Darwin blood." (The Darwins were notoriously unmusical.) Then he makes a joke about Emma's brother Hensleigh "think[ing] he has settled the Free Will question, but heredetariness [*sic*] practically demonstrates, that we have none whatever. . . . I daresay not a word of this note is really mine; it is all hereditary, except my love for you."

Annie is something. And then she fell ill. In *Darwin, His Daughter, and Human Evolution,* Randal Keynes, a Darwin descendant who had access to previously private family papers, makes the case, quietly and convincingly, that the view of existence that underlies *The Origin,* with its sober stoicism about the role of death and destruction in making new life, was shadowed by Darwin's experience of his favorite child's death.

She fell ill in 1850, with what seems to have been a form of tuberculosis, and her frantic parents spent months trying all the futile therapies that people had in the nineteenth century, not unlike the delaying actions of many contemporary cancer treatments. Darwin kept daily notes on her treatment, marking futilely that she was "poorly" or "little wakeful." He borrowed books for her, and since she was too weak now to read herself, he read them out loud to her. As he watched his favorite child sicken and suffer, he read Francis Newman's account of the transformation of his own faith, which turned, as those cases did so often in those years, on the meaninglessness of children's suffering, which seemed, seen close up, incompatible with the idea of a good God. (Keynes details at length the heartbreaking efforts Darwin made to keep his head by writing memos on Annie's failing.)

In the end, nothing helped, and Annie died at the age of ten, after a long vigil at a holiday villa in Malvern where Charles had taken her for comfort. Emma, who had to remain at home, got regular letters from her husband, each one sadder than the last. Finally he wrote, "My dearest Emma, I pray God Fanny's note may have prepared you. She went to her final sleep most tranquilly, most sweetly at 12 o'clock to-day." In her own diary, where Emma had been keeping track of the news from Annie's bed, she wrote merely "12 O'Clock."

Nothing really prepares us for the too soon loss of someone we love. Darwin had lost his father, and his mother, but nothing could have prepared him for losing Annie. It is like watching someone sink straight down into the waves, who will never return and never be recovered, while life continues on the surface. This sense, of the ongoing life of the world suddenly cut off irretrievably, of a life going on of which Annie no longer knows a thing, and in which her absence is absolute and permanent, is true grief—no memory can help it; no promise of meeting after can alter it. King Lear's "never's" are the horrible truth; once she was here, and she will never be again.

His sister-in-law Fanny, who was with him at Malvern, said that Charles had broken down, and cried for hours. Annie was buried at Malvern, but her father didn't attend the funeral. Heartbroken, Darwin composed a ten-page memorial and locked it in his desk. It is written in his best naturalist's manner: "She danced

well, & was extremely fond of it. She liked reading, but evinced
no particular line of taste. She had one singular habit, which, I
presume would ultimately have turned into some pursuit; namely
a strong pleasure in looking out words or names in dictionaries."
But the inventory was not unemotional. "She must have known
how we loved her," he concludes. "Oh that she could now know
how deeply, how tenderly we do still."

Within days he was back at work on his book, tackling one of
the hardest points in his theory, the absence of "intermediary
forms," the reality that between any two species we do not see,
either on earth or in the fossil record, all the many living things
that lay in between, and must connect them. He transferred his
affection to her sister Henrietta, who became his editor and assis-
tant and trusted first reader. She said that he hardly spoke of
Annie openly twice again in his life. And what remained of his
faith was dead too—and, more important, what remained of his
belief that he needed to show faith in order to keep faith with the
wife he loved.

All of these pressures—human and intellectual, the brave urge to
tell a new idea and the wise urge to tell it slant enough to have it
be mistaken for the old truths—were working on him as he sat
down, at last, in the late '50s, to write *On the Origin of Species*. All
the pleasures and pressures of the past decade acted on him: the
pleasure of explanation in simple terms, the pressure of not being
understood; the pleasure of having accumulated abundant examples, the pressure of succumbing to overabundant illustration; the
pleasure of having a clear argument to make, the pressure of having to make it clear; the pleasure of pushing at last to make a summary of an argument, the crucial pressure of having Alfred
Wallace, polite and deferential but, after all, also in possession of
the same theory, waiting. Above all, the pleasure of knowing that

the mystery of mysteries *could* be solved, basic truth found—and the pressure of knowing that parts of the truth would bring nothing but more grief to the one he loved most, and would leave forever in the dirt a child he loved. Truth had both to be said and to be softened, and at length.

The Origin is, as he explained after, the abstract of an abstract, a simpler version of the first contracted, then expanded version of his great work that he had been dreaming of in the '40s. He realized that he had to write a completely new kind of story, in a tone that would make it seem arrived at; he had to present dynamite as brick, and build a house, only to explode the old foundations. Long-felt speculation had to be presented as close-watched observation, and a general idea about life had to be presented as a sequence of ideas about dogs.

At the start of *The Origin,* after Darwin announces that he will study and treat the great problem of species—"that mystery of mysteries, as it has been called by one of our greatest philosophers"—there is a sudden deceleration of intensity. He devotes the first chapter to an exhaustive examination of the techniques of dog breeders and pigeon fanciers. A feeling of disorientation is followed by a rising sense of delight. We feel a bit as we do at the beginning of *Henry IV,* when we are told that the young prince has surrounded himself with dangerous companions—only to meet a fat old knight and his pathetic hangers-on.

Turning the pages, we realize that Darwin, the greatest Victorian sage, does not write like a Victorian sage. He writes like a Victorian novelist. Absent from his work is the pseudo-biblical rhetoric, the misty imprecations favored by geniuses of a more or less reactionary temper, like Ruskin and Carlyle, or the parliamentary ponderousness of the writers of a more or less progressive sensibility, like Macaulay and Arnold. Darwin's prose is calm and exact and, in its way, witty—not aphoristic, but ready to seize on a small point to make a large one, closer to George Eliot and

Anthony Trollope than to his contemporary defenders, like T. H. Huxley and John Tyndall. But then Darwin had a novelist's problem when he sat down to write: how to reconcile the endless variation of the natural world with a set of organizing patterns. ("Variation under Domestication," the title of the first chapter of *On the Origin of Species,* could be the title of the collected works of Eliot, as, for that matter, *Selection in Relation to Sex* could be that of Trollope's.)

On the surface, *The Origin* is a very strange book, a book designed to prove an ambitious thesis: that life has a single family, and that it all has changed over generations from simple forms to more complex ones by an unplanned winnowing out of new features through the competition among organisms for existence. It is not a survey of the field from a new point of view. It is, as Darwin said, "one long argument"—an argument with illustration, not a survey with instances. Everything is always varying; any variation that helps an organism eat better and have more sex will enable it to have more kids with the same feature, who will have more sex and eat better too, until the other, older kind of organism just dies out. Anything that helps in the struggle for existence will be saved. But it is an argument that reads like a story, not an abstraction applied narrowly to life but a commonality won from observation. Look at what these creatures are like! Look what they do! See how strange they are! Doesn't a single moral come to mind?

The point that Darwin wishes to make through the agency of dogs and birds, though not directly demonstrative of his thesis, is brilliantly illustrative of it. If a wolf—within a time frame so short that it can almost entirely be recorded, and by means so simple that they can be mastered even by illiterate people—could be transformed through selective breeding into everything from a Great Dane to a toy Pekingese, then surely Nature, working on a time scale so much greater, could produce even more dramatic transformations—say, monkey to man. Similarly, if one kind of pigeon can become all kinds of pigeons—some to deliver mail and others just to pout and look pretty—then one kind of animal could surely become many others as it descended through time and the pressures of specialized niches.

Instead of entering the argument by the front door of the temple, where people debate the origin of the earth and the destiny of man, Darwin, with an artless shrug, enters through the back door of a barn. Do we really know what happens when animals change? Well, yes, he says, and here's what we know, very exactly. Nor is this a mere gesture occupying a page or two ("one need only look at the rich achievements of the domestic breeder to see . . .") and pointing in a general way toward an acknowledged truth. Darwin offers instead a complex and exhaustive demonstration of how animal domestication and breeding work, by someone who has been in the shed with the birds and the eggs. We learn countless details about how pigeon fanciers change pigeons, and about how cattle vary in pasture. His immersion in the field enables him not only to make his primary point at length but also to make a critical secondary point: that even when domestic breeders aren't trying to vary their cattle, the cattle vary anyway, through isolation and inbreeding. Change happens when you want it to happen, and when you don't.

What's more, the proud domestic pigeon breeders, ignorant of biology, insist that each of their many breeds must derive from a unique species, even though biologists know that the many kinds of domestic pigeon arise from one common species, our old familiar Central Park friend. Darwin gently uses the biologist against the breeder, the breeder against the biologist. The climactic passage of *The Origin*'s opening chapter is at once innocently wide-eyed and scalpel-sharp, using the amused first person to make the central, impersonal point:

> I have discussed the probable origin of domestic pigeons at some, yet quite insufficient, length; because

when I first kept pigeons and watched the several kinds . . . I felt fully as much difficulty in believing that since they had been domesticated they had all proceeded from a common parent, as any naturalist could in coming to a similar conclusion in regard to the many species of finches, or other large groups of birds, in nature. One circumstance has struck me much; namely, that nearly all the breeders of the various domestic animals and the cultivators of plants, with whom I have conversed, or whose treatises I have read, are firmly convinced that the several breeds to which each has attended, are descended from so many aboriginally distinct species. Ask, as I have asked, a celebrated raiser of Hereford cattle, whether his cattle might not have descended from Long-horns . . . and he will laugh you to scorn. I have never met a pigeon, or poultry, or duck, or rabbit fancier, who was not fully convinced that each main breed was descended from a distinct species. Van Mons, in his treatise on pears and apples, shows how utterly he disbelieves that the several sorts, for instance a Ribston-pippin or Codlin-apple, could ever have proceeded from the seeds of the same tree. . . . May not those naturalists who, knowing far less of the laws of inheritance than does the breeder, and knowing no more than he does of the intermediate links in the long lines of descent, yet admit that many of our domestic races have descended from the same parents—may they not learn a lesson of caution, when they deride the idea of species in a state of nature being lineal descendants of other species?

A revolution in human consciousness is made from the self-deluding vanities of rabbit fanciers and poor Van Mons's obvious mistake about Ribston pippins. The argument is airtight, inescapable, and cunningly faux-naïf. Darwin uses empirical instances not inductively, to build proof, but infectiously, to weaken resistance.

Darwin's gambit of beginning with dogs and pigeons was almost too successful; one of the readers employed by his publisher, John Murray, recommended in his report on *The Origin* that the book would sell much better if it were all pigeons, without the weird speculative stuff that came afterward. Yet Darwin made the literary decision along with the practical decision—he knew that he was going to write his book, and he embarked on his program of pigeon fancying in order to help himself get started. The decision was both ethical and rhetorical: Darwin looked for evidence in the homely, the overlooked, the undervalued, and the artisanal. This enterprise of learning from the low—of making the mere naturalist and fancier into a peer of the scientist—was an effort to shift the sources of knowledge and models of thought.

In a revelatory book, *Pilgrim on the Great Bird Continent: The Importance of Everything and Other Lessons from Darwin's Lost Notebooks,* Lyanda Lynn Haupt has a mind-changing chapter on Darwin's relation to the "pigeon fancy," the largely working-class London and Birmingham pigeon-breeding enthusiasts with whom he studied, and from whom he learned much of what we read in the first part of *The Origin.* Haupt, a bird lover herself— good Darwinian writing continues to come from the edges as much as from the center of the field—points out how obsessive and complicated Darwin's relation to bird breeders was. "He traversed, with glee, a boundary clearly marked in both the social and scientific sands," she writes. He attended pigeon shows, sought out the prizewinning specialists, and then had his children help him as he bred his own flocks. "I am hand & glove with all sorts of Fanciers, Spital-field weavers & all sorts of odd specimens of the Human species, who fancy Pigeons," he wrote to a friend. He formed a close working alliance with a self-educated pigeon fancier named William Tegetmeier, the poultry editor for the naturalist journal *Field,* to the point that Tegetmeier claimed a partnership with him. (Darwin gently demurred.) This enthusiasm for the overlooked was not peculiar to pigeons. As Gerald Weissmann has argued in his remarkable essay "Darwin's Audubon," Darwin, against the grain of his time, chose to take Audubon, the American rogue artist and amateur bird collector, seriously, and not just as a source of information but as a model of truth seeking. He set out to widen the scope of what counted and who was allowed to count in science while seeming only to count heads and pigeons.

Admiring a scientist's prose, we usually try to humanize it by mapping the pattern of metaphor within it: look, Einstein was a visionary just like Keats. But the remarkable thing about Darwin as a writer is not how skillfully he uses metaphor but how artfully he avoids it. He argues by example, not by analogy; the point of the opening of *The Origin* isn't that something similar happens with domesticated breeds and natural species; the point is that the very same thing happens, albeit unplanned and over a much longer period. The notebooks and letters and earlier drafts show that analogies—not least the very idea of "selection," nature conceived as breeder—were powerful tools for him, as for anyone else, but it was part of his shrewdness to use them parsimoniously in his exposition.

To call this novelistic is not to assert a cosmetic likeness; it is to see how closely bound storytelling and truth seeking can be. Both Trollope and Darwin work in the mock-epic mode: the acts of very small and humble and comic creatures, archdeacons and earthworms, are shown to be not just illustrative of heroic and cosmic workings but an aspect of them. Trollope's Barchester is a smallish place, but its acts are not diminutive; every kind of passion and betrayal and tragedy can be found within those narrow provincial precincts. Archdeacon Grantly is a Greek hero and Mrs. Proudie as big as Clytemnestra if we pay them the right kind of attention. England's pastures are small, and its kennels cozy, but for Darwin they contain the keys to all creation. The delight that we take in the work of both is the delight we take in being shown the vastness of the cosmos in a tea bag. (Darwin's own motto of cautious empiricism, "It's dogged as does it," was drawn from a character in *The Last Chronicle of Barset*.) Yet the empirical overcharge never becomes a mere data dump. Darwin had the gift— the gift of any good novelist—of making the story sound as though it just got pushed out by the descriptions. The plot seems to grow out of his observations rather than being imposed by his will; in reality, the plot came first, as it usually does.

Gillian Beer, in her influential 1983 study *Darwin's Plots,* identified basic ideas about variation, purpose, and development that Darwin learned from his philosophical predecessors and shared with the novelists of his day. No one who has read Beer's book can ever read *Middlemarch* again without seeing it as a kind of mirror of, or practical application of, *The Origin*. (Darwin and George Eliot were friends, and once, out of curiosity, attended a séance together.) Darwin's writing, as much as Eliot's, takes speculative argument and makes it look like empirical record keeping. But the man in the notebooks, with his breezy provocations, keeps peeking out even from the work of the whiskered eminence. The book is one long provocation in the guise of being none.

Yet the other great feature of Darwin's prose, and the organization of his great book, is the welcome he provides for the opposed idea. This is, or ought to be, a standard practice, but few people have practiced it with his sincerity—and, at times, his guile. The habit of "sympathetic summary," what philosophers now call the "principle of charity," is essential to all the sciences. It is the principle, as Daniel Dennett says, that a counterargument to your own should first be summarized in its strongest form, with holes caulked as they appear, and minor inconsistencies or infelicities of phrasing looked past. Then, and only then, should a critique begin. This is charitable by name, selfishly constructive in intent: only by putting the best case forward can the refutation be definitive. The idea is to leave the least possible escape space for the "but you didn't understand . . ." move. Wiggle room is reduced to a minimum.

This is so admirable and necessary that it is, of course, almost never practiced. Sympathetic summary, or the principle of charity, was formulated as an explicit methodological injunction only recently. In some ways, of course, the practice is very old; we know what we know about the Gnostics because of what Christian writers tell us of their views before refuting them. But we can't entirely trust their account because their only goal is to make the other guy look bad by making his case look ridiculous. The principle of charity is to make the other guy's argument look good (before, of course, making yours look even better). It was not commonplace, either in Darwin's time or before. Mill, for instance, or Huxley, both press down on the sarcasm pedal even as they start to play the organ of their invention.

All of what remain today as the chief objections to his theory are introduced by Darwin himself, fairly and accurately, and in a spirit of almost panicked anxiety—and then rejected not by bullying insistence but by specific example, drawn from the reservoir of his minute experience of life. This is where we get it all wrong if we think that Wallace might have made evolution as well as

Darwin; he could have written the words, but he could not have answered the objections. He might have offered a theory of natural selection, but he could never (as he knew) have written *On the Origin of Species.* For *The Origin* is not only a statement of a thesis; it is a book of answers to questions that no one had yet asked, and of examples answering those still faceless opponents. (Years later, Wallace would write to Darwin urging him to take on Spencer's aggressive politicized term "survival of the fittest" in place of his "natural selection." Darwin calmly explained that the virtue of natural selection was that it was a sister phrase to "artificial selection," which everyone conceded, whereas "survival of the fittest" was awkward and might raise political specters.)

Darwin invented, cannily, a special, pleading, plaintive tone—believe me, I know that the counterview not only is strong but sounds a lot saner, to you and me both. And yet . . . The tone reflects his real state. He *was* worried about the objections, he *did* spend long days worrying about eyes and wings and missing fossils, and he found a way to articulate both the anxiety and the answers to it. Darwin tells us himself that he forced on himself the habit, whenever he came across a fact that might be inconvenient for his thesis, of copying it down and paying attention to it, and that this, more than anything else, gave him his ability to anticipate critics and answer them. The idealized notion of the scientist who seeks out "falsifications" has been mocked, and with good reason. (The usual response of the theorist who has predicted that all swans are white, when faced with a black swan, is not "Look, my idea is wrong!" but "You call that a swan?") But Darwin's long years in the domestic Eden had also been years in the wilderness, years when he had had the chance to brood in a solitary way on what might be wrong with what he was thinking. His objections to his own theory were strenuous but impersonal—or, rather, because they were self-made, they were offered in the same tone, and with the same rigor, as the positive doctrines. In the back-

and-forth of actual debate, as our grandfathers would have said, personalities intrude. In the back-and-forth of a self-made contest, both sides have a shot.

Darwin not only posits the counterclaims; he inhabits them. He moved beyond sympathetic summary to empathetic argument. He makes the negative case as urgent as the positive claims. There are two main objections that are still made to Darwin's theory, and he anticipated both: the argument from irreducible structure and the argument from intermediate form. What's striking is that Darwin anticipates arguments against his theory that no one had yet made—the argument from eyes, the argument from missing links—and that these remain exactly and almost exclusively the arguments that are still made against it. It's a really amazing piece of intellectual empathy, and of beating one's opponents to the punch. (And was Emma responsible? She wrote a little note in his first attempt to explain the evolution of the eye, "A great assumption." Did he use her afterward as a sounding board?)

Of the first objection, the argument that eyes could not have been made without purpose, he agrees: "If it could be demonstrated that any complex organ existed, which could not possibly have been formed by numerous, successive, slight modifications, my theory would absolutely break down." And that "to suppose that the eye, with all its inimitable contrivances for adjusting the focus to different distances, for admitting different amounts of light, and for the correction of spherical and chromatic aberration, could have been formed by natural selection, seems, I freely confess, absurd in the highest degree."

Of the problem of links—that there are few transitional varieties left on earth, few in the fossil record, and not many walking fish or ape-men—he allows that, though the fossil record is necessarily incomplete, one would expect to find "intermediate varieties" in "intermediate conditions." That is, since you find two species of similar birds separated by, say, a range of hills, you would expect to find intermediates between the two species in the range itself, and you don't. "But in the intermediate region, having intermediate conditions of life, why do we not now find closely-linking intermediate varieties? This difficulty for a long time quite confounded me." The tone is not one of nettled pettishness but one of disarmed candor: I recognize that I might well be wrong, and let me say what the wrongness would be. Although scientific theories imply their falsifications, they rarely list them. Darwin's does.

This was in part a pose, or to put it another way, a stance, a persona. Darwin in his letters is clearly not particularly respectful of the objections that were raised to his theory. But it was something more than canny; it supplies an inner voice, a sound of rational anxiety, a recognition of fallibility and of seriousness that gives his great book an oddly unbullying tone despite being a thrusting, far from tentative or timid argument.

The habit of sympathetic summary, of reporting an objection or contrary argument fully and accurately and even, if possible, with greater force than its own believers might be able to summon, remains since Darwin the touchstone, the guarantee, of what we call seriousness. Darwin's special virtue in this enterprise is that he had to summarize, sympathetically, views contrary to his own that did not yet exist except in his own imagination. His special shrewdness lay in making as large an emotional meal of the objections in advance as could be made; he preempted his critics by introjecting their criticisms. He saw what people might say, turned it into what they ought to say, and then answered.

This isn't the place, nor am I the writer, to enumerate the arguments that Darwin produced. They are the same arguments his defenders make now. In summary, the argument from eyes emphasizes structure over function: eyes are made of earlier, smaller, simpler eyes: a light-sensitive nerve is enough to begin the process, and many intermediate eyes exist. "In the Articulata, we can commence a series with an optic nerve merely coated with pigment, and without any other mechanism; and from this low stage, numerous gradations of structure, branching off in two fundamentally different lines, can be shown to exist, until we reach a moderately high stage of perfection." (This is his answer to his beloved Emma's reproachful "great assumption": it isn't an assumption; it's a fact.) Swimbladders have become lungs; "an organ originally constructed for one purpose, namely flotation, may be converted into one for a wholly different purpose, namely respiration." (Darwin turns out to have been wrong in the particular case, though the concept was right.)

Two key words are *merely* and *moderately*—the point is that dramatic change happens undramatically. The problem of missing links is met by the incompleteness of the fossil record, by the brief lives of the in-between, and by the reality of species that *are* intermediate in the sense that they are clearly reusing antiquated complex structures for new purposes, taking cash registers and turning them into doorstops: "Who would have ventured to have surmised that birds might have existed which used their wings solely as flappers, like the logger-headed duck (Micropterus of Eyton); as fins in the water and front legs on the land, like the penguin; as sails, like the ostrich; and functionally for no purpose, like the Apteryx." The beauty of the sentence lies in the ease of the writer's reach as much as in the clarity of his demonstration.

The point, always, is the power that Darwin lends to undramatic words: to *small* and *slight* and *varied*. The world is a mixed-up place; variation is the rule already. Darwin's point, again novelistic, is not that everyone is missing a dramatic unseen case but that everyone is missing the small, incremental meaning of animals and evidence pushed to the margins: the oddities of life, the loggerheaded ducks' awkward pace and the Pekingese's self-possession, the animals that cleverly reuse old devices and the flowers that are half male and half female, the blind spot in the eye, which we don't see that tells us more about how the eye evolved, how we do see, than some sight out on the horizon. Instead of arguing from first premises, Darwin argues from what his friend Sydney Smith called short views, the object near at hand. The proof lies in seeing the things in front of us freshly, as they are.

Evolutionary biologists no longer embrace the idea of a distinct natural class of transitional forms, though they still use the concept to talk about fossils that demonstrate a surprising evolutionary link between two very different kinds of animals. In a sense, everything is transitional, and nothing is. Dinosaurs are not intermediate forms on their way to being chickens, though chickens are what—well, one of the things that some—dinosaurs became. His arguments remain the arguments that are used today. Darwin learned to be disarming in the most literal sense; like Chaplin with a bully, he takes the club out of his opponent's hand, beats himself on the head with it, staggers a bit, shows that he can survive the assault, and then tosses the club out of the frame with a sideways kick, leaving the opponent with nothing to do but smolder like a silent-movie villain.

These are not just what professors would call rhetorical strategies, things that work. They are a circuit of feelings and implicit themes, of voice, that makes *The Origin* not just a monument in science but a monument in human thought and feeling. One senses the originality of mind, how the stormy, sarcastic, quick-witted Darwin we know from his notebooks and letters, who worked in "mental rioting," becomes the narrator we know from his book.

Behind a strong style there is always a human pressure. As Darwin worked on *The Origin* in the ensuing years, Keynes shows, he was haunted by Annie's death. In earlier musings, he had written of "the dreadful but quiet war of organic beings going on in the peaceful woods." But after Annie's death these words seem to have been inadequate. Now he wrote, "Nothing is easier than to admit in words the truth of the universal struggle for life, or more difficult—at least I have found it so—than constantly to bear this conclusion in mind. . . . We behold the face of nature bright with gladness, . . . we do not see, or we forget, that the birds which are idly singing round us mostly live on insects and seeds, and are thus constantly destroying life." It is this view of life that illuminates the famous passage at the end of *The Origin,* where Darwin writes of the "entangled bank [of existence], clothed with many plants of many kinds, with birds singing on the bushes, with various insects flitting about, and with worms crawling through the damp earth," all produced through the blind agency of natural selection. "Thus, from the war of nature, from famine and death, the most exalted object which we are capable of conceiving, namely, the production of the higher animals, directly follows," he went on. "There is grandeur in this view of life, with its several powers, having been originally breathed into a few forms or into one; and that, whilst this planet has gone cycling on according to the fixed law of gravity, from so simple a beginning endless forms most beautiful and most wonderful have been, and are being, evolved." At the end of *The Origin* Darwin feints toward reassurance, suggesting that life will "tend to progress" over time. But his insistent, immediately adjacent point is that the future in which that progress may happen will be like the past—a vast stretch of geologic time, unstructured by plan or purpose. "We may look with some confidence to a secure future of equally inappreciable length," he writes, and though the words *confidence* and *secure* provide cushioning, the plain sense is that there is no God or plan to interrupt a coming span of time beyond our control or even our imagining. It is the blank prospect that Larkin saw from his high windows: more grains of sand, and more shaking.

After Annie's death, Darwin abandoned the remaining vestiges of Christian faith, the last preference for even Unitarian theology, and became, essentially, a stoic. He believed that the contemplation of the immensity of time, and the repertory of feelings, was all that was left to us. There was no inherent meaning in Annie's dying at ten, except the recognition that mortality was the rule of existence; serenity could be found only in the contemplation of the vast indifference of the universe. It is a stoic's vision of the world and a father's elegy for a favorite child, taken for no reason at all save the world's fatality, defying the world in her happiness, gone for good.

CHAPTER THREE

LINCOLN IN HISTORY

BACK TO THE RUBBER ROOM, WHAT MIGHT THE WORDS MEAN?

WHERE THE ANGELS BEGAN

TANNER, A LIMB-SHORT SHORT-HAND MAN

WHAT WERE THE BETTER ANGELS OF OUR NATURE?

WHAT HAD CHANGED? • THE WAR AND A NEW CULT OF MEMORY

IN THE MOURNING STORE; NEW KINDS OF GRIEF

FROM VERTICAL TO HORIZONTAL, HEAVEN TO HISTORY

WILLIE'S DEATH IN 1862; IN THE MIDST OF LOSS WE ARE IN GRIEF

MOST VEXED OF QUESTIONS, LINCOLN'S FAITH

EARLY UNBELIEF, AND THE WAR—TURN TOWARD PROVIDENCE

THE ARGUMENT OF THE SECOND INAUGURAL

A DARKER VISION THAN WE KNOW • GOD'S WILL *WILL* BE DONE

LINCOLN IN SUMMER, THE SOLDIERS' HOME

LINCOLN, STANTON, AND THE PEACOCKS

TRACKING THE AGES, A SOURCE IN THE PARANOID STYLE

"HELP, ANGELS! MAKE ASSAY!"

THE PROBLEM OF LIBERAL VIOLENCE

A FINAL VISIT TO THE BEDROOM

B ut what did Edwin Stanton really say at Lincoln's deathbed? Having traveled this far along the road, you can, I hope, begin to get a glimpse of the kinds of worlds of feeling and implication that were at stake—or at least at play—in that anxious and overheard epitaph. Angels or ages? Confidence in the eternal life, which most people had believed credible until a few decades before? Or a new esteem for the power of history to make things happen and to act as the sounding board for our actions? These were themes that ran through the time, and marked the beginning of ours.

But it doesn't get us any closer to knowing what was really said. Setting out on the long trail of endnotes and footnotes, one is led to Jay Winik's book on the end of the Civil War, *April 1865*. His endnotes lead one, eventually, to *Twenty Days,* by Dorothy Meserve Kunhardt and Philip B. Kunhardt Jr., a well-made book of photographs from the 1860s, which in turn leads the reader directly to the ur-source of the angels. The unorthodox, heretical account of Stanton's words is actually much easier to "source" than the canonical and orthodox and familiar one: it comes from a stenographic record made in the bedroom that night by a young man named James Tanner.

Tanner was a corporal who had had both legs amputated after the Second Battle of Bull Run—he walked on peg legs—and lived in the house next door to the boardinghouse, Petersen's, where Lincoln was taken. Sometime that night, as Stanton was beginning to interrogate witnesses to the shooting, one of his generals appeared on the steps of the Petersen house and called out for someone who could write shorthand. Tanner heard him and hobbled down to take dictation. He spent the rest of the night beside the dying president.

Shorthand is one of the forces that were reducing the intensity of the rhetorical and oratorical society—the society of speaking—that Lincoln had grown up within. The habits of that society—the big political meetings, the multihour addresses, the picnics and the parades climaxed by speechmaking—would linger on for decades, as habits always do. (Nothing has so much stamina as a dated social ritual, as parents of postmodern teens going out on prom night can attest.)

The scene in the famous "rubber room"—because, again, in the endless prints and other popular images, the walls of the room expand constantly, pressed by the number of dignitaries who had to be included—was uglier than even the more faithful imagery shows. Lincoln's head wound was bleeding throughout the night, and the doctors had to remember to cover up the blood with fresh towels when Mrs. Lincoln, fallen into a grief from which she never really recovered, wandered in. Lincoln was laid diagonally across the too-short bed, knees up, and naked underneath the mustard plasters that had been placed on his chest.

Stanton took charge, dictating messages and taking evidence, with Tanner pressed into service as his secretary. At last, at 7:22 in the morning, Tanner writes:

> The Reverend Dr. Gurley stepped forward and lifting his hands began "Our Father and our God" and I snatched pencil and notebook from my pocket, but my haste defeated my purpose. My pencil point (I had but one) caught in my coat and broke, and the world lost the prayer, a prayer that was only interrupted by the sobs of Stanton as he buried his face in the bedclothes. As "Thy will be done, Amen" in subdued and tremulous tones floated through the little chamber, Mr. Stanton raised his head, the tears streaming down his face. A more agonized expression I never saw on a human countenance as he sobbed out the words: "He belongs to the angels now."

Note, though, that while Tanner presumably heard all this, he didn't actually claim (as is sometimes implied in the pro-angels literature) to have recorded it in situ, what with the broken pencil. Still, his account, the ur-source of the "angels" quotation, sounds fairly solid.

What would those angels have summoned forth to the "Lincoln men" standing by the president's deathbed? The imagery of angels seems to have entered Lincoln's own rhetoric for the first time when he was revising William Seward's proposals for his first inaugural. Seward, soon to be secretary of state, had, with what must have been maddening condescension, slipped the president-elect a letter detailing what he ought to say to the country. It included a vague, conventional reference to the "guardian angel" of the nation. Lincoln seized on that reference and turned it into one of his most memorable rhetorical inventions, the "better angels of our nature," which might yet keep the country from war. The force of the rhetoric is such that its meaning can still be a bit obscure: North and South would not go to war, Lincoln was arguing, because of their common sense of a shared past. Lincoln's own angels already belong to history, to the ages.

When Washington died, the imagery employed in the outpouring of memorial art was all angels—angels lifting his deathbed to the heavens, over and over, again and again. This imagery was surely understood to be in part just symbolic. But it retained its power. A deist invocation for Washington—"Now he belongs to the deity" or "returns to Nature"—is conceivable. But it is hard to imagine anyone referring Washington's legacy *only* to the ages, to history, and not to heaven at all.

What had changed things, made history matter so much, was the war. Lincoln's was not the only deathbed in which a man cut down by a bullet in the cause of the North became the subject of a disputed memorial, an argument for an epitaph, an uncertainty in summing up—it was only the most important one. The background to that little room where Lincoln lay dying was the war that had just ended. As the historian Drew Gilpin Faust has shown, disputes over what to do about the dead—what to say, and how to remember them, how to honor and recall them—had been part of the sour cultural fruit of the past four years. The scale of the killing between 1861 and 1865 had forced throughout the country a new cult of memory—a new set of social rituals, some rooted in the Bible but many intensely secular, the rituals of republican mourning. These rituals—the response to the mass killing, from military cemeteries, neatly rowed, to a taste for tight-lipped prose, to the embalming fluid developed at the time by Yankee ingenuity to preserve dead bodies on their way home from the battlefield—still run through our veins.

The war had been expected to be if not a romp, then at least a rout, but turned out to be a bloody war of attrition, in which defensive firepower so overwhelmed the offense that—at Antietam and Fredericksburg and the Wilderness—soldiers mostly just stood there and watched each other die. At Shiloh, in 1862, the battle cost something like twenty-four thousand casualties; Gettysburg, in 1863, claimed twenty-three thousand casualties on the Union side alone; the South lost somewhere between twenty-four thousand and twenty-eight thousand. By the spring of 1864, Grant's losses in slightly more than a single month approached fifty thousand.

The killing was horrifying in its suddenness: eighteen-year-olds were ripped apart at close quarters by minié balls, or shot down in the middle of normal drill by tree-infesting snipers. There is no pleasant way to die in battle, but presumably a Byzantine ax bearer or an Anglo-Norman longbowman in Henry V's train would have had some belief that his individual courage or resourcefulness could help him control the outcome. The Civil War battlefield was pure Russian, or Virginian, roulette; you walked out and prayed that your bullet didn't come up. S.H.M. Byers of Iowa remembered one terrible battle where "lines of blue and gray" stood "close together and fire[d] into each other's faces for an hour and a half."

Organized massacre—men advancing to their deaths through close rifle fire—was the rule of battle, chaotic massacre the rule of its aftermath. The war had not been a neat epic of blue and gray but four years of terror and cruelty and violence. (With all the gallantry of an Einsatzgruppe on the eastern front, the gentlemen of the South set about killing black soldiers indiscriminately. "Private Harry Bird reported that Confederates after the Battle of the Crater in 1864 quieted wounded black soldiers begging for water 'by a bayonet thrust.' . . . Bird welcomed the subsequent order 'to kill them all'; it was a command 'well and willingly . . . obeyed.' General Robert E. Lee, only a few hundred yards away, did nothing to intervene.") After Antietam, a Union surgeon reported, "The dead were almost wholly unburied [and] stretched along, in one straight line, ready for interment, at least a thousand blackened, bloated corpses with blood and gas protruding from every orifice, and maggots holding high carnival over their heads." The rotting dead turned blue, then black. "Not a purplish discoloration, such as I had imagined in reading of the 'blackened corpses,' so often mentioned in descriptions of battlegrounds, but a deep bluish *black,* giving to a corpse with black hair the appearance of a negro," a Gettysburg veteran observed.

To deal with these horrors, a new set of social rituals, designed not so much to "blind" survivors to the reality as to make them believe that the reality was necessary and noble, had come into being. The work of mourning became the business of capitalism, merchandised throughout a society. In the spring of 1863, Lord and Taylor in New York, down on Ladies' Mile, opened a "mourning store," where the new widows of the Civil War could dress their grief in suitable fashion. Some idea of what they shopped for is apparent from the inventory advertised by Besson and Son, in Philadelphia, a mourning store of the same period: "Black Crape Grenadines—Black Balzerines—Black Baryadere Bareges—Black Bareges." The national mourning store included, of course, inspirational poems and high rhetoric, along with that new practice of embalming with zinc chloride, which "marbleizes" flesh and allowed some of the dead, at least, to travel home for burial in recognizable shape. (There was a secondary market in icebox coffins, for the same purpose. An advertisement was inserted in the Gettysburg paper soon after the battle for "transportation cases": "Preserves the Body in a natural and perfect condition . . . for any distance or length of time.")

Amplifying the new rituals, and democratizing them, were the recent inventions of the telegraph and the photograph. The telegraph meant that news of a battle, with the terrifying "lists," was available in a timely way. One hadn't consigned one's son or husband to a hades on earth from which he might or might not emerge years later; one would know, and soon. For the soldier, there were new kinds of photographs—tintype, daguerreotype, ambrotype—that made those left behind more real and constant; many soldiers died clutching photographs of their families. One of the most storied deaths of the war was that of Amos Humiston, a Yankee soldier felled at Gettysburg, who was found with an ambrotype of three children in his hands but no other identification. "The ultimately successful effort to identify him created a sensation, with magazine and newspaper articles, poems, and songs celebrating the devoted father, who perished with his eyes and heart focused on eight-year-old Franklin, six-year-old Alice, and four-year-old Frederick," as Drew Faust writes. In an irony that the postmodernists would appreciate, Humiston was most famously commemorated, clutching that photograph, in a *Frank Leslie's Illustrated* woodcut.

All of this was taking place within the larger tide whose force we've seen already in the lives of both Lincoln and Darwin, a changing belief in the centrality of family life—the same social forces that had led the Lincoln family, over one generation, from log cabin to big bourgeois house. Unlike the European practice of war, where peasant and proletarian infantrymen—largely detached from their families, who had long since given them up to the army and its institutions—and a tiny cadre of professional officers fought professional battles with a professional code of soldiering, in the American Civil War the soldier was often embedded in an ongoing family life. He hadn't enlisted as a teenager and then been lost to the Continent and the empire. He had gone to fight in Virginia for Ohio or Pennsylvania. His parents and siblings were waiting for him. The Civil War took place in a time, and in a country, where "modern" feelings of attachment to the immediate family were not just ascendant but aggressively honored, more, perhaps, than anywhere else. The ancient facts of battlefield death had to be parsed not as the medieval vestige they in some sense remained in Europe but within the grammar of the bourgeois life that surrounded them. In *Vanity Fair,* the Battle of Waterloo is both a social event and an aristocratic game, played for high stakes; when Amelia's husband dies, it is a risk taken in a risky life. By contrast, in *Little Women,* that matchless novel of home front life in the North, the March girls regard their father's war service not as a gamble but as a sacrifice.

The discontinuous nature of the Civil War in relation to all the other imperial bloodletting of the time—the extraordinarily high cost of the war and, at the same time, its extraordinarily high stakes—was apparent even to distant observers. Charles Darwin himself wrote to his American friend Asa Gray in 1862, speculating that the war might be better settled than fought. Gray had sent Darwin a newspaper article on the war, which, Darwin said, "we read aloud in Family conclave. Our verdict was, that the N. was fully justified in going to war with the S.; but that as soon as it was plain that there was no majority in the S. for ReUnion, you ought, after your victories in Kentucky & Tennessee, to have made peace & agreed to a divorce."

Yet Darwin also understood clearly the cost of *not* fighting the South. Slavery in his mind was such a "hopeless curse" that, if the war could mean an absolute end to slavery—by no means an entirely clear end or ambition of the North's in 1862—"I would then run the risk of your seizing Canada (I wish with all my heart it was an independent country) and declaring war against us" (that is, against the British). And no one put the real stakes of the war more clearly: "I can see already it [the Civil War, and the North's ill success] has produced wide spread feeling in favour of aristocracy & Monarchism: no one in England will speak for years in favour of the people governing themselves." What was at stake was the continuance of liberal democracy, the popular will tempered by law as a working ideal, a practical goal.

A true fault line in modern consciousness exists in those years, and can be found beneath Lincoln's deathbed, as it can be found beneath so many other beds. For in these years—for the first time, and despite much conventional religious piety—there's a nascent sense throughout the liberal world that the deaths of young men in war will never be justified in the eyes of a good God, and never compensated for by a meeting in another world. Their deaths can be made meaningful only through a vague idea of Providence and through the persistence of a living ideal.

Part of our sense of Lincoln's moral grandeur lies in our belief that Lincoln understood this. Lincoln was an executioner, and nothing we can say can diminish his responsibility for death and killing on a massive scale. At the same time, while Lincoln grasped the "awful arithmetic," in his famous phrase—the scale of the killing, and the brutal reality that the North could lose men and keep on fighting and the South could not—he also grasped the scale of dying, the scale of the national grief. That's when we see him wandering through the White House, hands clasped behind his back, saying, "What will the country say?"

Lincoln's speeches as the war goes on echo the general transformation in the country: from a neat punitive morality to a search for a historical point in the slaughter. That is the change marked in his words at Gettysburg, where the self-sacrificing soldiers are martyrs not to religion but to a new birth of freedom. For the first time, fewer people found comfort in the promise of eternal life; more found it in the idea of a new world worth making. It was here that the real shift, exemplified in our little dualism of the A's, is felt. It wasn't a small shift. For most of history, ordinary people lived their lives vertically, with reference to a heaven above and a hell below. Now we live our lives horizontally, with reference to future generations for whom our sacrifices and examples may make a better life. (We live horizontally, too, in the knowledge of sex and death as shaping principles.)

This change had been visible for a while. Whitman wrote about it before the war in terms largely approving and enthusiastic. "I am," he explained:

an acme of things accomplished, and I an encloser of things to be.
My feet strike an apex of the apices of the stairs,
On every step bunches of ages, and larger bunches between the steps,
All below duly traveled—and still I mount and mount.

. . . .

Before I was born out of my mother generations guided me,
My embryo has never been torpid . . . nothing could overlay it;

. . . .

the long slow strata piled to rest it on . . .
vast vegetables gave it sustenance,
Monstrous sauroids transported it in their mouths and deposited it,
    with care.

This is touching, if unintentionally funny—the image of Whitman's embryo being daintily borne in the mouths of dinosaurs is one that Thurber alone could have drawn. Yet it is the same idea—the idea of man placed in history in a way that compensates for any loss of divinity he might experience. *On every step bunches of ages*—with history at your feet, who needs God on your side?

The Civil War was one place, in America certainly the key place, in which this change got made—no longer as a blessing or an advance but not entirely as a loss either. At the end of the war, the rituals were not merely secular but in their quiet way antireligious, grounding the meaning of the war entirely in the sublunary realm of gains and losses, in history, in the ages.

And, like Darwin, Lincoln knew death through the death of a favorite eleven-year-old child. In the winter of 1862, Lincoln's son Willie fell ill with what seems to have been typhoid, contracted, most probably, from the untreated polluted water that flowed in Washington. Willie (like Annie a decade before) had become obviously, and fatally, ill in a short time. Lincoln, as president, had three sons, but Robert, the eldest, though loyal and brave, seems to have been intellectually shallow in a way his father found alien, and the baby, Tad, was, as would be said now, "somewhere on the spectrum."

It is often said—more often than one might imagine—that nineteenth-century people, because they suffered so many more child deaths than we do, felt them less, or differently, than we might think—or made less of a fetish of them or, because they sometimes photographed bodies, had a set of expectations and rituals for child death radically different from our own. As we've seen in the case of the Darwins' mourning, there is no evidence for this at all—just the opposite, actually. Their loss was as complete as ours would be, and their grief as deep. If anything, their grief was deeper, because their shock was less. There was no surprise to buffer it, no sense of a million-to-one shot to place it in the realm of things that never happen. It was not a brick that fell on your head from a skyscraper but the one thing you had always actively dreaded. (Parents during the polio era would resonate with that same emotion.)

Certainly that was the case with the Lincolns when Willie died. By a painful coincidence, Willie's illness struck just as Mary Lincoln was arranging a grand White House ball meant to be a kind of social "coming out," and she went back and forth, dazed, from ballroom to sickroom. After a long up-and-down battle, Willie Lincoln died, drowned by his own fluid, on February 20. "Well, Nicolay, my boy is gone—he is actually gone!" Lincoln sobbed to his secretary, and then went into his own office, weeping inconsolably. ("I never saw a man so bowed down with grief," said the woman who helped dress and wash the dead boy and then watched his father look at his face one final time.)

Of course it is possible, using the dry ice of some kind of false historical consciousness, to "universalize" the Lincolns' loss in the larger losses of the time. It is even possible to find something strange, or tasteless, in Lincoln's grief for his own son's death at a moment when he had sent so many other sons to their graves. Many boys were gone. But for Lincoln, the national experience of death had no real traffic with—offered no "perspective" on— his loss, which belonged to his own irreducible core experience. This space between the common experience of death in battle and the core experience of loss and grief remained unbridgeable by any shared rite. Death was everywhere, death was omnipresent, death was necessary to preserve the people's government, and might very well be dignified by genuine idealism and a belief in the necessity of sacrifice; Willie's death was no different to his parents than the deaths of all those other, slightly older boys who were dying every day were to theirs—but these thoughts provided no pause in the pain. Lincoln's loss was at home, not on the field (though his son Robert did fight). But the central experience of his time—that is, the inability to see death as a preface to immortality but instead to feel it fully, as unappeasable loss—was his, too. After Willie fell mortally ill, Lincoln may have turned to the Bible. It would have been unusual if he had not. But we know that he turned to Goethe, taking the German poet's *Faust* from the Library of Congress. And he is said to have spoken to Rebecca Pomroy, an army nurse who had been brought in after Willie's death to help Mrs. Lincoln look after Tad.

> She says, "I told him I had a husband and two children in the other world, and a son on the battle-field." "What is your age? What prompted you to come so far to look after these poor boys?" She told him of her nineteen years' education in the school of affliction, and that after her loved ones had been laid away, and the battle-cry had been sounded, nothing remained but for her to go, so strong was her desire. "Did you always feel that you could say, 'Thy will be done?' "
>
> And here the father's heart seemed agonized for a reply.
>
> She said, "No; not at the first blow, nor at the second. It was months after my affliction that God met me when at a camp-meeting."
>
> . . . Then he told me of his dear Willie's sickness and death. In walking the room, he would say: "This is the hardest trial of my life. Why is it? Oh, why is it[?]" I tried to comfort him by telling him there were thousands of prayers going up for him daily. He said, "I am glad of that." Then he gave way to another outburst of grief.

Lincoln sought for a religious understanding of his loss, but seems not to have achieved it; glad for prayers, he did not find prayer itself sufficient. The consolations of the camp meeting, the surety of the "other world," intrigued him without completing him. (Even in Mrs. Pomroy's story, whose lugubrious details some historians have doubted, thinking them more likely a creation of the post hoc sentimental Lincoln than of life, Lincoln hears, but does not second, her faith in the other world.)

The most affecting stories from the Civil War are of people who, as Lincoln did, came to recognize this duality: accepting the fact of death, unable to reconcile themselves to its justice in the eyes of a good God—believing in the goodness of the cause and still finding nothing in the mourning store that fit, ignoring the usual circular, vertical rituals of church and sermon, the rituals of domes and heavens and angels, and trying to improvise flat, horizontal rituals, the new rituals of homes and history and ages, to make sense of what remained intolerable loss.

There is, to place alongside the president, Henry Ingersoll Bowditch, for instance, whose son Nat died in Virginia in 1863 after being left wounded on the battlefield. Grief stricken, the father tried the usual cant of consolation: he listened to sermons; he read inspirational poetry. Nathan, he told himself, died for a great cause; he had "died happily"; he was waiting, as the preachers insisted, "just the other side of the veil." None of it helped; it was, historically, too late for that. "My heart seems almost breaking," he said simply, and he couldn't turn his mind from his loss. At last, he made a monument for his son in the shape of his sword, and to "get out of myself" he crusaded for better ambulance service on the battlefield, the kind of thing that might have saved his son's life. There was no comfort to be found, but there was work to do, no pride in death, merely unending sorrow and the possibility, some distant day, of meaning.

Lincoln's whole life and "aura" show him sensitive to the alteration in mourning and its meaning. But how did Lincoln himself resolve the struggle? What epitaph would he have chosen had he had a moment to choose? The question of Lincoln and the angels leads to the most vexed question in all the Lincoln literature, that of his faith. How religious—how willing to credit more than metaphoric angels—did the men in the room think that Lincoln was? It is vexed because the evidence points to two truths, difficult to reconcile. On the one hand, Lincoln was all his life—aggressively in his youth, more mildly in his age—anti-clerical and anti-dogmatic, not any kind of churchgoing Christian but a profound and declared skeptic. In his first campaign for Congress, he admitted that he was not a member of any church and that "in early life" he had argued for the "doctrine of necessity"—that is, a belief in man as a mere pawn of universal law, without free will.

Both Mary Lincoln and Lincoln's Springfield law partner, William Herndon (also his first major biographer), were unequivocal about his rejection of any standard churchgoing faith, and the various posthumous claims that he "converted" to some form of Christianity have been mostly exploded. Herndon, who surely knew Lincoln better than did any other man, wrote, "He firmly believed in an overruling Providence, Maker, God and the great moral of Him written in the human soul. His—late in life—conventional use of the word God must not by any means be interpreted that he believed in a personal God. I know that it is said Mr. Lincoln changed his views. There is no evidence of this."

Yet, undeniably, as the war and his presidency progressed, Lincoln, as Herndon knew, did speak increasingly of God—inserted God, as it seems, into the Gettysburg Address—and evidently had some kind of complicated and rich sense of "necessity" and a supernatural presiding power. Oddly, it is a form of belief closer to that of the Old Testament, where God's will is assumed and his strange purposes deduced through human suffering, than to the deism of the Enlightenment, where God's good purpose is assumed to emerge through the ultimate balance of pain and pleasure, and human suffering serves a larger purpose. Job knows that he is suffering for no good reason; what he learns is that feeling pain and being the subject of "good reasons" have nothing to do with each other. There is no justice that we earn, but there is fate that we share.

The historians' literature on Lincoln's late faith and his late style is rich and growing, but the best studies are perhaps by those whose expertise is in the way words work as much as in the way minds change. Three of the best twentieth-century students of American literature addressed the question of Lincoln's faith, and how it got expressed in his writing and speaking toward the end of his life. The now insufficiently appreciated Van Wyck Brooks wrote in the 1940s that with the mature Lincoln, "the intensity and depth of his conviction, the religious nature that had led so many in the Western country, at a time of signs and wonders, to regard him as a patriarch Abraham returned in the flesh." Lincoln's conceptions, in this view, were deliberately Old Testament— "patriarchal." Frankly unbelieving though he might have been, in his tone, his example, "he had reached a positive faith that was much like Whitman's, a religion of humanity that Jefferson had shared with them and that flowed through many Americans, through Emerson and through Melville. In all that Lincoln said and wrote, behind it, underneath it, ran the deep river of feeling that ran through Whitman."

For Edmund Wilson, writing fifteen years later in his *Patriotic Gore,* this notion of an American religion of humanity, applied to the man who had pursued and prosecuted this bloody war, was sentimental and foolish (though Wilson blamed Carl Sandburg more than his friend Brooks). He admired Lincoln no less, but admired him for the taut austerity of his vision, and of his prose— an Old Testament vision to be sure, but one not of a wise patriarch but of an avenging tribal priest, sure of himself and hard, and anticipating, in the severities of his speechmaking, the "chastened," subdued style that Stephen Crane and Grant alike would learn. Wilson's Lincoln came from a sordid childhood, began in a boorish backwater, and by sheer force of purpose became "intent, self-controlled, strong in intellect, tenacious of purpose." Wilson grants that "[Lincoln] must have suffered far more than he ever expressed from the agonies and griefs of the war" but sees his last speeches as expressions of a tough philosophy of "historicizing" nationalism—the nation is the true unit of meaning in the world, it reveals itself in history, and it must be baptized in blood.

Alfred Kazin, as so often, with his extraordinary gift for emotional reading, for entering sympathetically into the mind and real concerns of the writer, hit a note more moderate and yet accurate: Though lit by Calvinist fatalism and frontier evangelical enthusiasm, Lincoln's view of divinity and providence was original. Lincoln, contemplating the scale of death, and the evil of slavery, and sensing the hand of God in both, came to the realization that "since it all happened as described . . . one can only yield to the enigma of having such a God at all. It is clear that the terrible war has overwhelmed the Lincoln who identified himself as the man of reason. It has brought him to his knees, so to speak, in heartbreaking awareness of the restrictions imposed by a mystery so encompassing it can only be called 'God.' Lincoln could find no other word for it." For Kazin, Lincoln's God is neither the God of confident Christendom nor the punishing God of the Calvinist imagination but the God of both Job and John Donne, the God who is the stenographic name for the absolute mystery of being alive and watching men suffer while still holding in mind ideals that ennoble the suffering and in some strange way make sense of it. As Donne wrote, "Tribulation is treasure in the nature of it, not current money in the use of it."

(A sense of the other side's view of the same issue, expressed with considerable asperity and irony, comes from General Edward Porter Alexander, the Confederate chief of ordnance at the Seven Days. Lincoln, he tells us, was right; the South *did* think that God was on its side. "It is customary to say that 'Providence did not intend that we should win,' . . . [but] Providence did not care a row of pins about it . . . it was a serious incubus upon us that during the whole war [Jefferson Davis] & many of our generals really & actually believed that there was this mysterious Providence always hovering over the field.")

The second inaugural is the most famous instance, and the key statement of Lincoln's mature vision and of the style he had invented to articulate it. Crowded by his own conditionals— his great speech at Gettysburg and the second inaugural are sequences of *if* clauses:"if one accepts the proposition that . . ."— in the second inaugural, too, he begins, as he had done so often as a younger man, with dry, polite talk—"The progress of our arms, upon which all else chiefly depends, is as well known to the public as to myself and it is, I trust, reasonably satisfactory and encouraging to all. With high hope for the future, no prediction in regard to it is ventured"—only to turn to monosyllables as he explains his history of what has happened in the past four years: "But one of them would *make* war rather than let the nation survive and the other would *accept* war rather than let it perish. And the war came."

And the war came. It's a sentence that Harold Ross would not have allowed in the old *New Yorker* (because it isn't exactly a sentence and begins with *and,* a false connective). But it is as precise a gesture as you could ever have, with a biblical inflection, and does the work of making the war's arrival seem providential, natural, rather than causal—with the effect of deflecting responsibility from one side or another while making it a great catastrophe from which all sides must recover together. (Maddeningly so, for both the Southern slavery nuts like Booth who were listening and the Northern abolitionists, who knew that the war hadn't come but was made.) It is a lot of work for four monosyllables, but it did the job.

He then enters into an argument essentially legal in its form—as he had at Gettysburg and as he always had since 1838—not an exhortation of principle but a close-made argument of conditionals. If this is so, then this must be so; stipulate this premise, and this conclusion follows. The argument of the second inaugural—which, like the argument at Gettysburg, feels so familiar that it is hard for us to grasp how complicated it is—is that if we accept what God knew to be the evil of slavery into the world, and into America, for some mysterious purpose but with a definite lease, intending to end it, and if God made the war so horrible in order to punish those who brought the evil into the country (notwithstanding that God deliberately failed to prevent them from doing it in the first place), then does this strange equation make us believe less in a God capable of acting so bizarrely? Well, no, Lincoln says, even if that were so, "still it must be said 'the judgments of the Lord are true and righteous altogether.'" This is Job's language, the language of mystical resignation: it makes no sense; it has happened; there must be a purpose for it because without it all would be senseless slaughter—so there must be a God. It is not the neat argument that God balances all but that nothing is balanced and yet God, somehow, remains. Lincoln isn't simply saying that the war is the national payment for the sin of slavery, which will end as slavery ends. He is saying that the war is willed by fate for reasons that we cannot fully know but that must have something to do with the balancing scales of long historical time.

For atheists, like the young Lincoln, this was not a challenge; necessity moved all. For the older Lincoln, overwhelmed by the core experience of grief, of death in the family, and the common experience of so much death in war, the idea of a universe moved only by necessity was too painful—the absence of a God had become so intolerable that one had to be evoked even as his purposes were seen as enigmatic. That is why we find the insistence that "if God wills that . . . [the war] continue until all the wealth piled by the bondsman's two hundred and fifty years of unrequited toil shall be sunk, and until every drop of blood drawn with the lash shall be paid by another drawn with the sword, as was said three thousand years ago, so still it must be said 'the judgments of the Lord are true and righteous altogether.' "

This is a darker vision of Providence, and of God, than is quite compatible with any kind of ordinary Protestantism. In a review of James Tackach's *Lincoln's Moral Vision,* Lucas E. Morel writes, "Lincoln's perplexing piety comprised a fiercely independent admixture of Enlightenment rationalism and Calvinist fatalism." His faith was rooted mainly in a kind of mystical inner sense of predestination, not so far from that youthful doctrine of necessity. He found no serenity in the idea that he was doing God's work. His point in the second inaugural is not that he is doing God's will but that God's will is going to be done, no matter what Lincoln does. He thought not that God was on his side or the other but that God had determined on this conflict, perhaps as a collective punishment for the sin of slavery, perhaps for reasons permanently mysterious to men.

He came increasingly to believe in Providence, but it was a Providence that acted mercilessly through history, not one that regularly interceded with compassion. That was left to men, and presidents. His idea is unmistakably "spiritual," the conception of someone who believes in a shaping power, a divine power, but not in an interceding divinity, a good Father. It is Chambers's doctrine of necessity evolved, so to speak, into a form of fatalism—the faith that the universe moves forward turned into a belief that battles make men better.

Lincoln's last position, ironically, is not entirely unlike that of his close watcher and sometime admirer Karl Marx—sublimation of Old Testament fatalism into a new religion of history, where history does the brute, necessary work of nation building through the extended punishment that Jehovah had done before. The proletariat or the Union soldier might be martyred for the good of the cause, racked but made central by history much as the Israelites had suffered for the glory of the nation, suffering but chosen by God. Lincoln's religion is closer to Marx's than to the sunny self-congratulation of his claimed successors now. The difference, a vital one, is that Lincoln did not believe that he was the prophet of that history, standing astride it; he was its witness, acting within it, of course, but also just watching in wonder.

The one place in America where you can get a sense of Lincoln the president at work and at play is in the Soldiers' Home, on the outskirts of Washington, about three miles from the White House. After the death of Willie, in 1862, Lincoln used a cottage on the grounds as a kind of retreat, a proto–Camp David, and spent summers there from 1862 to 1864. Every other place associated with him either predates the presidential years or has changed so much that it is unrecognizable. But Lincoln's cottage, which has been largely neglected, still resonates with the period. It was an odd location for him: though it was cooler than central Washington in the summer, it was also a soldiers' retirement home, with a cemetery just alongside, where Union dead were sent to be buried.

Lincoln loved the Soldiers' Home, preferring it to the stolid White House. Walking through the buildings, one sees that the rooms have a nineteenth-century spaciousness and ease, and one is reminded that, as Richard Carwardine points out, the young Lincoln was avid as much for bourgeois respectability as for riches, or even for fame. It was in these bright but cozy rooms, too, and out on the surrounding lawns, that he and Stanton really took the measure of each other.

The story of Stanton and Lincoln—the reason that, at the very last moment, the deathbed assembly deferred to Stanton to say the final words—is well retold by Doris Kearns Goodwin and, in particular detail, by William Lee Miller. In the 1850s, Stanton had been a prominent litigator, and in 1855 he and Lincoln were thrown together in a complicated patent litigation with an Illinois angle. Lincoln felt that here at last was his opportunity to break into big-time law. He prepared maniacally, only to find himself, at the trial in Cincinnati, shuffled off by the senior Stanton and prevented not only from arguing but even from consulting with the senior lawyers. Lincoln didn't hold the incident against Stanton, a Democrat whose contempt for him, even after he was nominated for president, was almost open, and made him secretary of war after his first choice, Simon Cameron, got caught up in a scandal.

At the Soldiers' Home, Lincoln and Stanton became friends. They shared a common tragedy—both had lost a son in the course of the war—and a common nature, outwardly remote, inwardly passionate. (When Stanton's young wife died, he insisted on having a wedding dress made for her to be buried in, and for months he wandered through their house, half mad, crying out for his bride.) Stanton, too, had a cottage at the Soldiers' Home, and spent summers there with Lincoln. Most people intensely disliked Stanton; one cabinet secretary called him "rude and offensive." But at the Soldiers' Home, as Matthew Pinsker shows in his book *Lincoln's Sanctuary,* another side of his nature became apparent: he played mumblety-peg with a soldier and, on one memorable occasion, spent an evening with Lincoln untangling peacocks. (Small blocks of wood had been tied to the birds' feet with strings to keep them from flying away, but the lines had got snarled in the trees.) As Stanton came to know Lincoln, he formed an opinion of his intellect so high that he said to one of his fellow lawyers, "No men were ever so deceived as we at Cincinnati." It was a friendship deep enough, and famous enough, to make everyone in Lincoln's last room wait for Stanton to speak.

Though it is easy to track the exact source of the revisionist "angels," it is much harder to find the source of those "ages." Like many famous scenes and remarks, it entered memory through a window while no one was looking. When, in 1890, John G. Nicolay and John Hay, Lincoln's two secretaries, wrote what was to be for almost a century the standard life of Lincoln (whom they called the Tycoon, seeing him as a politician of limitless shrewdness rather than as a saint of infinite patience), the entire atmosphere of the death scene had changed and, with it, the words. Their Stanton coolly breaks the silence of death and pronounces his benediction: "Now he belongs to the ages." Hay was certainly in the room, near the deathbed, and knew the people involved far better than Tanner could have, and his account is crisp and definitive sounding.

But where before then had it been registered? The trail of footnotes leads one eventually to the most thorough account of how Stanton's words entered the American memory, and it occurs, bizarrely, in Otto Eisenschiml's 1937 book *Why Was Lincoln Murdered?*—bizarrely because Eisenschiml, whose book was a best seller in its day, was a conspiracy theorist who believed that Stanton had conspired to have Lincoln assassinated. (His motive was supposedly to gain a harder peace for the South than Lincoln would have allowed, though there is no evidence that they disagreed on this point.) Eisenschiml, forgotten now, was an original, a German-born chemist turned amateur historian who helped invent the style and model of a certain kind of American paranoia: the by-now familiar fussing over odd but irrelevant inconsistencies (Stanton seems to have had enough testimony to identify Booth shortly after midnight on the night of the murder, but he didn't release Booth's name until later that morning—because, of course, he wanted Booth to escape, and so on) and the same patterns of sinister coincidence (Oliver Stone claimed that the telephone lines went down in Washington after Kennedy's murder, and sure enough, Eisenschiml believed that the telegraph lines were deliberately cut in Washington on the night of Lincoln's assassination).

Yet paranoid obsession can be a spur to close study, and Eisenschiml took the trouble to find out when "ages" might have entered the imagination. Once again, there is a wildly varying set of memories. Lucius E. Chittenden, who had worked for Lincoln in the government, claimed that what Stanton actually said was "There lies the most perfect ruler of men the world has ever seen!"—although he was not at Lincoln's bedside. One of Stanton's clerks, also not present, insisted that he said, "Ah, dear friend! there is none now to do me justice; none to tell the world of the anxious hours we have spent together!" But in the twenty-five years that separated the scene and Hay's version of it, the record is cloudy. None of the newspaper reports in the days following the assassination, though all contain scenes from the deathbed, mention the words. (Eisenschiml imagines that Stanton's having been reported as saying "angels" would have been a disaster—too self-consciously pious—and that he spread the "ages" story afterward. "Perhaps he told it to eager-eared hostesses," Eisenschiml sneers.) Charles Sabin Taft, one of the attending doctors who had been in Ford's Theatre, wrote in notes that he claimed to have made the following day (but did not publish until twenty-eight years later), "When it was announced that the great heart had ceased to beat, Mr. Stanton said in solemn tones, 'He now belongs to the Ages.'" But Taft's father also kept a diary (it is available online), and in recounting the scene as his son described it to him, he makes mention of neither ages nor angels.

Hay put his stamp on the words as we usually hear them. That was adequate warrant for a century, and perhaps should be still. He was there; he had no plausible motive to lie and no reason to misremember. It is possible that there is an obscure source for the epitaph in the twenty-five years between the event and the biography, but the famous words seem remarkably fragile, insecurely sourced and late in arriving, like so many other moments in history that seem sure until they are inspected, and become more uncertain the longer they are sought.

The effort to give shape and meaning to the bleak horrors of the Civil War can be seen in the rituals of mourning, but it can also be seen in the war's literary relics. Emily Dickinson and Ambrose Bierce are not "representative" of anything; if they were, they wouldn't matter. But, as Wilson saw and as Louis Menand has reminded us, there's a sense in which the strange, astringent, skeptical tone that they distilled from the war is revealing of the era's search for ritual and rhetoric. Walt Whitman is the one figure in whom this double movement—toward the war as a noble enterprise, away from all war as horrific slaughter—is conscious and complete. He was writing rote letters of condolence to the families of the dead even as he was working on his great war poems in which the suffering, far from ennobling, simply doesn't end:

> The living remain'd and suffer'd, the mother suffer'd,
> And the wife and the child, and the musing comrade suffer'd,
> And the armies that remain'd suffer'd.

A republic of suffering is made of infinite islands of mourning; we form the archipelago afterward, and only in our minds.

All of these literary changes would happen at the war's end, and in the decades after. But there was already available for Lincoln and his circle a tragic rhetoric, a heartbreaking set of words, a style of persuasion and self-understanding richer than the others. For there's another rhetorical style that runs like the Mississippi right down the middle of the mid-nineteenth-century American mind, shaping phrases and supervising thoughts, flowing as strong as the classical, the biblical, and the lawyerly, and that is the Shake-spearean. Lincoln's love of Shakespeare is familiar but is usually treated as a delightful character trait, like his fondness for ice cream or the comedy of Artemus Ward.

The influence of Shakespeare's rhetoric and rhythms on Lincoln might have been already the secret to his practice of summary in monosyllables. It is a Shakespearean habit—almost, as Barry Edelstein has written, a Shakespearean mode. In Lincoln's favorite *Macbeth* alone we can find, at or near the end of speeches: "nothing is but what is not," "false face must hide what the false heart doth know," and "I go, and it is done," all of them culminating short-footed gestures.

But Lincoln's taste in Shakespeare was narrow, significant, and almost obsessive. He didn't love *A Midsummer Night's Dream* and *As You Like It;* it was the histories and three of the tragedies that held him. In 1863, he repeatedly went to see *Henry IV* when James H. Hackett was playing Falstaff, with all the Falstaffian black comedy against conscription and the cult of honor. He took volumes of Shakespeare out of the Library of Congress, went to a Washington theater to see the famous E. L. Davenport in *Hamlet,* attended private recitations of Shakespeare, sought out a production of *Othello,* watched Edwin Booth, John Wilkes's brother, in *Richard III,* and the greatest American Shakespearean, Edwin Forrest, in *King Lear,* at Ford's. Just five days before the assassination, on April 9, 1865, steaming up the Potomac in the presidential yacht, he spent "several hours" reading aloud from Shakespeare to those on board. Reciting from his favorite plays was a weakness of his; on August 22, 1863, Hay records in his diary that he fell asleep at the Soldiers' Home while listening to Lincoln recite Shakespeare.

In a letter to Hackett, Lincoln admitted, "Some of Shakespeare's plays I have never read; while others I have gone over perhaps as frequently as any unprofessional reader. Among the latter are 'Lear,' 'Richard III,' 'Henry VIII,' 'Hamlet,' and especially 'Mac-beth.' I think nothing equals 'Macbeth.' "These are all dramas of unexpected murder, of ambition turned into evil. Many writers have commented on how strange and naked it is that Lincoln, who, as his partner Herndon wrote, ran relentlessly on the "little engine" of his own ambition, should have embraced a tragedy about ambition. He was plainly haunted by the imagery of fallen and ruined leaders, and sensed how fine a line separates a king and a usurper, or a Lincoln and a Davis.

But even stranger and more striking is Lincoln's identification or, at the very least, fascination with the figure of Claudius. In that same letter to Hackett, Lincoln insisted that Claudius's soliloquy beginning "O, my offence is rank" was superior to any of Hamlet's, and we know that he committed it to memory, and would recite it at length even to acquaintances—an artist who had come to paint his portrait, for instance. Lincoln's evaluation was as unorthodox then as it is now. And what is the burden of Claudius's speech? It is about guilt and ambition, and about the fraternal blood dealing that that produces. As Kenneth Tynan pointed out, Claudius's tragedy is that he is clearly the most able man in Denmark, but he has got his throne through blood and cannot be free of the taint. (No one, except Hamlet, criticizes his conduct as king.) His speech runs through the difference between his conduct as seen on earth and in heaven and ends with an image of his soul as a "limed" bird, caught in a sticky trap, that gets more stuck as it struggles:

> *"Forgive me my foul murder"?*
> *That cannot be; since I am still possess'd*
> *Of those effects for which I did the murder,*
> *My crown, mine own ambition, and my queen.*
> *May one be pardon'd and retain the offence?*
> *In the corrupted currents of this world*
> *Offence's gilded hand may shove by justice,*

And oft 'tis seen the wicked prize itself
Buys out the law: but 'tis not so above;
There is no shuffling, there the action lies
In his true nature; and we ourselves compell'd,
Even to the teeth and forehead of our faults,
To give in evidence. What then? what rests?
Try what repentance can: what can it not?
Yet what can it when one can not repent?
O wretched state! O bosom black as death!
O limed soul, that, struggling to be free,
Art more engaged! Help, angels! Make assay!

There's no reason to believe that Lincoln "identified" with Claudius, or thought his own conduct evil. But he shuddered to think what his ambition, together with his principles, had helped make happen. He recognized and understood the pain of one who, believing himself to be essentially good and capable of salvation, as Claudius does, knows that he is covered with blood—one who, having chosen to take on the weight and worry of the world, knows that he has done it and, like Macbeth, too, cannot be free of its guilt: *Help, angels! Make assay!*

What makes Lincoln still seem noble, to use an old-fashioned word, is that he had not a guilty sense of remorse but a tragic sense of responsibility. He believed that what he was doing was right; he knew that what he was doing was dealing death to the undeserving (knowledge that must have been doubled at the Soldiers' Home as the bodies were brought to be buried week after week). If Lincoln truly has something in common with Jesus, it is that he is the model of a charismatic ethical intelligence who was also a calm dealer of punishment on a vast scale: *Some to my right and some to my left . . .*

Lincoln exemplifies the problem of liberal violence: the disjunction between the purity of our motives (as they appear to the liberal) and the force of our violence (as it is experienced by the victim). The reality of his faith in his beloved rule of reason, and the constant presence of his magnanimous and winning character, doesn't preclude his engagement in mass killing—*the corrupted currents of the world*. (That other autodidact midwesterner, Harry Truman, also turned to *Hamlet* to find words to expiate his blood-guilt, underlining at the end of a book about the atomic bomb a long quotation from the last act that begins, "Let me speak to the yet unknowing world / How these things came about: So shall you hear / Of carnal, bloody, and unnatural acts, / Of accidental judgments, casual slaughters, / Of deaths put on by cunning and forced cause / And, in this upshot, purposes mistook / Fall'n on the inventors' heads.")

Lincoln's spiritual state by the end of the war was very much like that of a Shakespearean tragic hero: resigned to a deadly fate that he did not will but would not avoid. Shakespeare's continuing appeal to liberal societies, despite his feudal settings, is in many ways strange. Shakespeare's beliefs are wide, but they always turn on questions of hierarchy, degree, legitimacy, and on medieval virtues, too: charity, mercy, laughter—all of the things that redeem and lubricate and soften a hierarchical system. He is a skeptic, like Montaigne. But he is not in any sense modern; skepticism is the liberalism of the powerless. It gives one the right to doubt the perfection of the king without doubting his necessity.

But there's another sense in which Shakespeare's people and their poetry anticipated the modern condition. His stories are of ordinary ambition, admirable in itself, turned in against itself after being bathed in blood. Bolingbroke is a better man for king than Richard II, but Richard's killing leads Henry to his long night; even Othello, innocent victim of the malignant Iago, and Lear, innocent victim of his own cruel children, have put themselves into false positions, raised above their place or abdicating too soon. The little engines of ambition in Shakespeare almost always crash, and when they find their way to their destination, as Henry IV does, they end up crashing anyway. Shakespeare's people pass from ambition to amorality to evil in one long gradient of gray; only a moral idiot would be sure that his gray days were not part of the same sad declining curve. Part of Shakespeare's genius lies in his ability to create characters who intend no harm and end up covered with blood. And so Shakespeare suits liberal violence, with its corrupted currents, admirable ambition, and casual slaughters— and what makes Lincoln and Truman admirable, if not heroic, is that they knew it.

After a long time spent thinking about what had been said, and what it meant, I decided at last to visit the Petersen House, the tiny old boardinghouse in Washington, where Lincoln spent his last hours. I stood in a long line stretching out to the door, surrounded by other tourists, waiting to get to the room at the back where Lincoln died. Now, after months of reading, I was convinced that the first thought that would have crossed Stanton's mind was the angels. Given the man, and the association, what else but angels? Though perhaps they would be not so much the religious angels of an ascension as the Shakespearean angels of fate, the ones who wear us out, the angels whom Claudius prayed to and who sang to Hamlet at his end.

And then, later, someone—perhaps Stanton at the time, or perhaps only Hay long afterward—thought that there was more point and solemn originality in what someone else (Hay from the very moment perhaps?) thought he had heard, and decided to change it. As the line shuffled forward, I made up my mind about what must have happened: Stanton had muttered "angels," had been heard as saying "ages," and, if he had been asked which afterward, would have been torn. He might have decided to enable the mishearing in order to place Lincoln in history, not heaven. It seemed possible that both versions were true, one to the intention and the other to the articulation, one to the emotion of the moment and one, in retrospect, to the meaning of the life. Angels or ages? Lincoln belongs to both.

The sentence forms in the mind, and with it the thought that there would be a good place to end: *he belongs to both*. But as the queue inches forward and I can see, at last, into the room that I have been reading about—I want to laugh. This place isn't small; it's *tiny*. They brought him here, to this back room, I had learned, because all the other rooms in the house were too messy for a president to die in, and yet—*four* people would make it crowded; six would overwhelm it; the forty or so who passed in and out, and the ten or twenty who crowded inside at the end, would have turned it into the stateroom scene in *A Night at the Opera*.

In the brief moment given to a visitor to look inside, I wished for a machine that would be able to re-create every breath of air, every vibration that ever took place in a room. And then I knew that we probably would not have understood any better had we been standing there then than we do now. Stanton was weeping, Lincoln had just died, the room was overwhelmed, whatever he said was broken by a sob—the sob, in a sense, is the story. History is not an agreed-on fiction but what gets made in a crowded room; what is said isn't what's heard, and what is heard isn't what gets repeated. Civilization is an agreement to keep people from shouting "Fire!" in a crowded theater, but the moments we call historic occur when there is a fire in a crowded theater, and then we all try to remember afterward when we heard it, and if we ever really smelled smoke, and who went first, and what was said. The indeterminacy is built into the emotion of the moment. The past is so often unknowable not because it is befogged now but because it was befogged then, too, back when it was still the present. If we had been there listening, we still might not have been able to determine exactly what Stanton said. All we know for sure is that everyone was weeping, and the room was full.

CHAPTER FOUR

DARWIN IN TIME

D arwin's *Origin,* when it was published at last, in November of 1859, was a hit. The first printing sold out (though whether it actually sold out or the remaining copies merely disappeared among previous orders isn't clear—a difference that every author knows to be significant. It struck with an overwhelming splash). Later, Darwin's obituary in the *Proceedings of the Royal Society* of London would say, "It is doubtful if any single book, except the 'Principia,' ever worked so great and so rapid a revolution in science, or made so deep an impression on the general mind. It aroused a tempest of opposition and met with equally vehement support."

Yet the really striking thing, given how radical his great idea really was, is how mildly that tempest passed. The general response, though obviously accented by firecrackers of indignation, on the whole ranged from welcoming and enthusiastic to skeptically respectful. "Overflowing the narrow bounds of purely scientific circles, the 'species question' divides with Italy and the Volunteers the attention of general society," Huxley wrote a year later. And:

> Everybody has read Mr. Darwin's book, or, at least, has given an opinion upon its merits or demerits; pietists, whether lay or ecclesiastic, decry it with the mild railing which sounds so charitable; bigots denounce it with ignorant invective; old ladies of both sexes consider it a decidedly dangerous book, and even savants, who have no better mud to throw, quote antiquated writers to show that its author is no better than an ape himself; while every philosophical thinker hails it as a veritable Whitworth gun in the armoury of liberalism; and all competent naturalists and physiologists, whatever their opinions as to the ultimate fate of the doctrines put forth, acknowledge that the work in which they are embodied is a solid contribution to knowledge and inaugurates a new epoch in natural history.

The railing was mild, and the last clause, certainly true, was the most important. Other naturalists had read it, and got it.

As always in life, good luck played a role. Right away, in

December of 1859, Huxley had been able to insert an anonymous review of the book in the London *Times*. Huxley, who was quick and rhetorically gifted in a way that Darwin did not pretend to be (but genuinely modest in his submission to the stronger if milder mind of his friend), praised the book with what is, in retrospect, surprising if strategic caution, admitting that it is possible that Darwin may have "been led to over-estimate the value of his principle of natural selection, as greatly as Lamarck overestimated his *vera causa* of modification by exercise"—that is, Lamarck's belief that giraffes, by stretching their necks to eat from the top branches of trees, pass on longer necks to their children. But Huxley had got not only the theory but also the nature of the argument, and pressed it on this crucial audience:

> But there is, at all events, one advantage possessed by the more recent writer over his predecessor. Mr. Darwin abhors mere speculation as nature abhors a vacuum. He is as greedy of cases and precedents as any constitutional lawyer, and all the principles he lays down are capable of being brought to the test of observation and experiment. . . . If it be so, it will carry us safely over many a chasm in our knowledge, and lead us to a region free from the snares of those fascinating but barren Virgins, the Final Causes, against whom a high authority has so justly warned us.

Huxley understood that Darwin's argument was an argument against "the final causes." On the question of species, he announced right there in the *Times,* at the height of a Victorian Christmas season, that you could never again appeal to mysterious authority or ultimate purpose; you could appeal only to rational argument and the specific case.

It is hard, I think, to overestimate the importance of this review in the *Times,* so soon after the book's publication, for Darwin's state of mind. In the letter he wrote to Huxley right after the appearance of the review, in which he coyly kept up the pretense of not being able to imagine who wrote it, Darwin exults: "Who can the author be? I am intensely curious. . . . Certainly I should have said that there was only one man in England who could have written this essay, and that *you* were the man. But I suppose I am wrong. . . . Well, whoever the man is, he has done great service to the cause. . . . The admission of such views into the Times, I look at as of the highest importance, quite independently of the mere question of species."

One feels the palpable level of anxiety drop off for Darwin in this letter; that anxiety, which dominates his letters of the 1850s, never returns, and a new tone of mocking, ironic confidence takes its place and remains. For the rest of his life, Darwin, though often exasperated by his correspondents' demands and exhausted by his illness, never sounds *worried.* Even when important doubts were raised about his theory—was the earth old enough to have sustained so much change? wouldn't changes in animal inheritance tend to blend together?—he found a way to fight back, and the words to fight back with. Darwin exults in 1859 because he knows what anyone engaged in a controversial enterprise wants to know—that, whatever the opposition, there will be strong allies and high praise on his side, making the fight tolerable and even fun. His fear, not unreasonable, had been that the whole thing would be blasted out—wrongly, but such things happen— and that he would have to fight uphill all the way. Because of his allies, and because of a bit of luck—the *Times* in London, the *Thunderer,* held, as Trollope illustrates in his novels, the kind of power on social issues that the *Times* in New York still has on Broadway, making and closing shows—the thing was well launched. From that moment on, though he would be attacked and in doubt about details, he would never doubt that the vision he had had in 1838 was fundamentally persuasive to fair-minded men. Educated people in 1859 were already saying that it *might* be so, though probably not. And when they start saying that it *might* be so, the point is carried.

Contingency counted, luck helped, the zeitgeist was there to be taken. Far from speaking to readers who would find his work a shocking violation of the norms, Darwin wrote for an audience already in many ways becoming nonreligious; according to the religious census of 1851, less than half the population of Britain was attending church or chapel. The work (or damage) of disbelief had already largely, and long before, been begun by Hume and Gibbon and the "higher criticism" of the Bible. The old bones and the new books had done their business.

But Darwin's own carefully wrought strategy of persuasion was still surely key to the book's reception. He had written a book whose tone of empirical exactitude, fair-minded summary, and above all, sweeping argumentative force—so subtly orchestrated that it acted not as a straitjacket on the argument, pressing it in, but as a tide behind it, driving it forward—was almost impossible to resist, even if one doubted the claim.

Huxley, in fact, himself given to hardier and more conventional polemical outbursts, was a bit exasperated by what he saw as the woolliness and near diffidence of Darwin's argument, complaining in the *Westminster Review* that "notwithstanding the clearness of the style, those who attempt fairly to digest the book find much of it a sort of intellectual pemmican—a mass of facts crushed and pounded into shape, rather than held together by the ordinary medium of an obvious logical bond." Had Huxley written *The Origin,* it would have mocked more, shone less. Had the logic been made as obvious and "philosophical" as Huxley wanted—as obvious as Huxley himself tried to make it in his own polemical defenses of Darwin—it would have been less nourishing and sustainable in the long run. Pemmican is good food for long journeys.

For the next quarter century Darwin and Huxley continued to

play, knowingly, a kind of good cop–bad cop game in public. Their correspondence shows that each knew his given role—when Darwin at last was put forward for an honorary degree from Oxford by the reactionary Lord Salisbury, it was with the severe corollary that Huxley could not get the same. Huxley and Darwin, sharing the same basic views, enjoyed the joke. When Huxley had his famous debate with Bishop Wilberforce, Darwin kept silent, safe in the country, but wrote to his defender, "How durst you attack a live Bishop in that fashion? I am quite ashamed of you! Have you no reverence for fine lawn sleeves?" And then: "By Jove you seem to have done it well!"

Darwin's gift as a natural novelist is the secret to the book's persuasiveness; his eloquence is marshaled in the guise of a story inhabited by creatures, not a polemic made by one man. It *was* an argument, but it was also a narrative—not "Here's what I think is the secret of life," but "Here's how this story must have happened." Gillian Beer has diagrammed the many and deep resemblances between Darwin's writing and the "evolutionary plots" of contemporary Victorian novelists, particularly those of his friend George Eliot. This parallel need not defer only to the zeitgeist or the immediate friendship for its force. In a famous, much misunderstood passage in his autobiography, Darwin insisted, modestly, that as he grew older, he found himself lacking in aesthetic feeling but then goes on to say, at once, how much he still loved reading novels. One can miss the point entirely if one imagines that Darwin is saying, with a sigh, that he can read only scientific papers; what he's saying is that he finds it harder to go on reading *Idylls of the King* in preference to *Middlemarch* and *The Prime Minister.* He is showing good judgment, not literary indifference. Victorian novels, though now rightly known as one of the high points in the history of writing, and civilization, were a pop form in his time; no special aesthetic credit accrued to one who read them. Darwin's point, modestly put but insightful all the same, was that a scientist could find a satisfaction in the close crawl observation of Victorian prose that he might not find in the higher flights of Victorian poetry.

Like the novelists, Darwin appealed to a cross section of Victorian readers. It is a gross oversimplification, to the point of parody or falseness, to imagine that Darwin appealed especially to one or another part of the Victorian world—to free marketers, who saw the invisible hand of the market extended to nature; to industrialists, who saw the bitter system of factory competition reproduced in every pond; or for that matter to nascent Marxists, who saw in it a model of sweeping historical explanation; or, despite what Huxley says, even to liberals, who saw intimations of freedom in between its paragraphs on chance.

In truth, he appealed about equally to almost everyone who could search and find in his theory a metaphor for his pet project. Radical atheists found radical atheism in it; Marx found his own sense of historical action without conscious intention within it; yet devout Christians could find a more than adequate theological consolation in it as well. One copy of *The Origin* that Darwin inscribed and signed before publication was for Charles Kingsley, the eccentric but devout English clergyman and poet-writer who had been made Queen Victoria's chaplain in 1859. Kingsley, a very odd man—he once wrote Darwin a pre-Freudian letter about how much religious hostility to sex depended on the excretory and reproductive functions of man being placed so closely together—wrote his somewhat Joycean children's classic, *The Water-Babies,* in the light of both Darwinian theory and the Bible. By "regularizing" nature, by making the history of species as explicable as the path of the stars, Kingsley thought, Darwin had revealed the hand of God in earthly pattern, had joined biology to astronomy and physics and all of the other fields that had already, in the hands of theologically minded men, shown divine order where before there had been only willful impulse. Darwin himself appears in *The Water-Babies,* a humble and unworldly figure, head in the clouds, pockets filled with fish and fossils—the sort who couldn't harm a fly, or a fair-minded theologian. So the first response to *The Origin,* primed by Darwin himself, is a form of mystical Christianity.

Of course, Darwin's ideas came out of the light of his day—in what other light could they have been made? But his mind was a prism; the light of his time changed crucially as it passed through, and showed a new and different spectrum. The analogy linking Darwin's ideas on nature with free market ideas on nations, for instance, though still insisted on by his largely brilliant biographers James Moore and Adrian Desmond, is surely forced. There *are* resemblances between Darwin's theory of what has been called a "blind watchmaker" who governs natural selection and Adam Smith's doctrine of an "invisible hand" that governs markets. The likeness lies in the idea of a system that has order and pattern without agency, that works efficiently and even elegantly without anyone's having designed it: I buy a house; you buy a house; we put up a fire station to keep me from burning down your house, and we hire a policeman to keep you from burgling mine, and next thing you know, wanting nothing but our own selfish good, we have a neighborhood and a city. In the same way in nature, a frog eats a bug; the next frog who happens to have a longer tongue comes along and eats more; the greenest of the bugs being preyed on hide best against the lily pads, and before you know it, we have long-tongued frogs attempting to eat ever-greener insects in an ongoing little lily pad world. Organization emerges without the interference of planning. The natural city isn't "zoned."

But the differences between nature and the market in time scale and intention are much greater than the resemblances. Adam Smith's invisible hand is really the concerted action of a thousand small acts of calculation; Darwin's great sorter is the cumulative result of a thousand blind acts of copulation. Animals in evolutionary biology don't want to extend their family line, to produce progeny or improve, or even extend, their species; they just want to get laid. The variation that may result—the longer-tongued frog, the greener bug—is, quite literally, a lucky bastard. No male salmon impregnates salmon eggs with the idea of making more salmon. (Not even every human group knows that sex will lead to offspring.) There is a difference between an invisible hand and a blind watchmaker. One is the result of the immediate interacting of human intentions; the other, of the long-term accidents of animal lust. (No animal, even an Icelandic one, ever sleeps with another organism in order to improve the species.) Greed is good because personal prosperity almost always becomes general; sex is not good *because* it improves the breed. Sex is sex, and the breed gets better by chance and time, by the oddities of random mutation and the winnowing of natural selection.

In this way, Herbert Spencer and the rest of the right-wing Darwinians misread *The Origin,* and tried to insert will into a natural system that, in Darwin's view, didn't have it. They wanted Nature to have a purpose, a point, and a plot, not just a history. On the other edge, Karl Marx was just as impressed by Darwin as Spencer was. The story that Marx wanted to dedicate the second volume of *Das Kapital* to Darwin seems to be false; Darwin wrote to him politely, following the publication of the second German edition of *Das Kapital,* that "though our studies have been so different, I believe that we both earnestly desire the extension of Knowledge, & that this is in the long run sure to add to the happiness of Mankind." But Marx went ahead and, imitating Darwin as he understood him, tried to drain all will and purpose from the human system of politics that *did* have them. By insisting that History will work out its dialectic independent of our acts, just as Nature shapes forms independent of the individual organism's experience—that the most we can do is midwife changes that are anyway bound to happen—his version of Darwinism encouraged a contempt for active political reform in favor of heightening the contradictions and waiting for the revolution to come. Marx, too, has an insistent eschatology, a sense of the direction and arrow of history, that is alien to Darwin. Darwin thinks that many terrible things happen in nature but not that history is moving toward a Utopia in which no animal will ever again eat another.

And so a Darwinian "left" and a Darwinian "right" were both in place before most people had grasped the Darwinian middle, which was where the maker was. The Victorians got so much metaphoric resonance from *The Origin* because it was unique in having a double charge, a double dose of poetic halo. It is both an explanation of evolution, an old idea, and a theory of natural selection, a new one. If you concentrated on the evolutionary part, which is, as Darwin knew, an old and long-present idea, one of Granddad's tall tales, then you could make it into a kind of pro-gressivism—an explanation of eternal change and social improve-ment with a vitalist charge. If you concentrated on the natural selection part, the struggle for survival, you could make it into an endorsement of free markets or imperialism or anything else you liked. The real point, which Darwin understood and was clear about, was that the book got its charge where the two ideas com-bined to make a third, entirely new one: that things that look fine-tuned by engineering can be made by the compounds of accident, ages, lust, and hunger. Natural selection made whales just as artificial selection made Pekingese and greyhounds, and it turned monkeys into men just as breeders turned wolves into lap-dogs. Natural pianos are made by unnatural patience.

Scientific ideas become a whole climate of opinion when they can provide a set of metaphors for people who aren't doing science. Darwin, like Einstein, certainly provided the metaphors, though, like Einstein, he hadn't intended to. People thought that natural selection might prove that Britain was powerful because nature intended it to be, as they thought that Einstein's relativity might imply that anything goes at a party. (In fact, the point of natural selection is that Nature doesn't play favorites, just the odds, just as Einstein's relativity is special because there's something in it that *isn't* relative, the speed of light, which is absolute. It would make more sense for us to become sun worshippers in the light of Einstein than moral free-for-allers.)

Yet morals and metaphors aside, the most important way in which Darwin altered his era was by getting people who *did* do science to ask a new kind of question. Some scientific revolutions have surprisingly small ideological aftershocks; Michael Faraday's discovery that electricity and magnetism are the same thing was as large a discovery as any in the history of science, but it had a paltry aftereffect. We don't talk about Faradayism, or about Faradayan economics (though there's no reason why somebody couldn't equate economic waves, in their pulsating pattern, with electromagnetic ones). For a new scientific theory to become a model in its time, vastly influential outside its immediate claims, it has to release thinking people from a bond that they had long recognized as too narrow and help them interrogate the world in a new way. What *really* matters is not that the answers suggest a new metaphor for amateurs but that it shows a new kind of question to other pros. Other scientists have to say not, "How smart of him to discover that," but "How extremely stupid of me not to have thought of that! If only I'd stopped to ask . . ."

As a small boy, for instance, I was a witness to the Chomskyan revolution in linguistics (in which my mother and, later, my sister both played parts). In retrospect, what Chomsky proposed are in truth fairly specific ideas about language and the way it's learned, which solved some problems and led to others—but the broader metaphoric aura, the poetic charge, was to release a generation from the narrow bribe-and-threat model of learning that behaviorism, in place before in the field, had insisted on, and make space for new inquiry. Now psychologists and linguists and philosophers felt free to ask questions about what was there in the mind, about innate ideas and blossoming modules—entering inquiringly a previously forbidden garden of inbuilt mental structure—rather than ruling those questions out of court from the start.

The power of the new Darwinian questioning was everywhere apparent at the time. All over Europe, biologists and naturalists began to ask *why* rather than *what* questions about life. It was revolutionary science that proposed "normal" science, things to do. It still is potent today, even to us amateurs. Walking in Central Park at twilight, impregnated with the Darwinian ether, you suddenly ask yourself why there are fireflies in Italy and the eastern United States but not in California, on the Pacific coast? I don't know the answer to this, but I know Darwin would have asked it. By always asking questions that ran against the taxonomic grain—asking not, what *is* it? but, what's it related to? and, how does it make a living?—he immediately altered the world.

Addendum: A little research reveals that fireflies in fact do exist on the other side of the Rockies—but that the ones that crossed the mountains, while anatomically like our glowing little guys, are for the most part not bioluminescent: they fly, but they don't fire! Which leads one quickly to the Darwinian speculation that flashing fireflies must have made themselves too visible to unknown sharp-eyed predators they hadn't faced on the eastern side of the mountains—only a desk-bound speculation, but one surely worth pursuing if only to disprove. It also turns out that fireflies are bewilderingly hard to classify, for precisely Darwinian reasons: they're so compacted that it's very hard to tell varieties from species. Asking pre-Darwinian questions—essentially, to what place in nature does this thing belong?—quickly dissolves into questions of words and names, while asking instead Darwinian questions—how does this thing make a living? what will it leave its children? how does it pay for the house? and what villain is trying to foreclose on its mortgage?—pays off in less fixed, and more interesting, answers.

In an odd way, John Stuart Mill, whose *On Liberty* used Darwin's reluctance to publish as an argument for tolerance, may have eaten the social marrow of the theory better than anyone else. His argument for liberty wasn't just, or especially, for the brave Giordano Brunos of the world, who speak scientific truth in the face of the Inquisition and the fire. It was also for the oddballs. It is desirable, he wrote, for people to be "eccentric": "Eccentricity has always abounded when and where strength of character has abounded; and the amount of eccentricity in a society has generally been proportional to the amount of genius, mental vigor, and moral courage which it contained." The idea that odd sorts and variations were to be valued for the sake of progress, that bizarre variation was the key to the growth of knowledge, may have been a more truly wise extension of the Darwinian idea to human social life than any other in its day.

You could plausibly read into Darwin pretty much any politics you wanted, left or right, socialist or laissez-faire, liberal or radical, Christian or freethinking. The one thing that you could not read into Darwin's writings was racism. Or, rather, you could, but only by simple misreading—not by freely interpreting what the book *might* say but by falsely declaring what it *did* say. The story of what came much later to be called "social Darwinism," with its racist and "eugenic" beliefs, is a long and sad one; it has a lot to do with the social life of the late nineteenth century, and little to do with Darwin or his actual ideas. Darwin is insistent that there are no original differences among people, that all human beings belong to a single family, and that all have the same kinds of roots and the same kind of mind. At a time when religious bigots are trying to undermine the teaching of evolutionary biology in America by calling Darwin a racist, this cannot be said loudly enough, or often enough, or clearly enough.

Darwin argues, in *The Descent of Man, against* Archbishop Whately, a leading theologian whose "On the Origin of Civilization" had embraced the view that the lower races had "fallen away" from God. "It may be doubted," Darwin writes, "whether any character can be named which is distinctive of a race and is constant. Savages, even within the limits of the same tribe, are not nearly so uniform in character, as has been often said. . . . The most weighty of all the arguments against treating the races of man as distinct species, is that they graduate into each other, independently in many cases, as far as we can judge, of their having intercrossed." (That is, they descend from the same fathers even if they haven't all slept in the same bed.)

Again in *The Descent,* he writes, "Although the existing races of man differ in many respects, as in colour, hair, shape of skull, proportions of the body, &c., yet if their whole organisation be taken into consideration they are found to resemble each other closely in a multitude of points. Many of these points are of so unimportant or of so singular a nature, that it is extremely improbable that they should have been independently acquired by aboriginally distinct species or races." People are different, in Darwin's view—he thought there were savages, primitives, at one end and civilized people at another—but what knit them all together was the habit of sympathy, which could be extended wherever, and as far as, we chose to place it. "As man advances in civilisation, and small tribes are united into larger communities, the simplest reason would tell each individual that he ought to extend his social instincts and sympathies to all the members of the same nation, though personally unknown to him. This point being once reached, there is only an artificial barrier to prevent his sympathies extending to the men of all nations and races."

We should not judge the past by the standards of the present. Darwin wrote about "savages"; we wouldn't. (But then, we use words that our great-grandchildren will be shocked by, too—though which ones: *wife? veal chops?*) But we should not judge the past by the standards of the past either—if we did that, we'd smile politely as some of our ancestors burned books, and nod understandingly as others burned witches (and some of us would be nodding as both our ancestors *and* their books got burned). We should judge the past by the standards of the best voices that were heard within it. Shakespeare's anti-Semitism in *The Merchant of Venice,* ugly as it is, occurred in a time when no one had a clear idea of what Jews were, and of what anti-Semitism actually was. Jews were about as real to Elizabethans as Orcs. The modern anti-Semitism of the great but flawed genius G. K. Chesterton, on the other hand, can't be defended by saying that "everyone thought that way then" because not everyone did. (By 1920, the only people who did were anti-Semites like him, and a chorus of the decent was there to tell him, loudly and at length, that it was shameful. It was his choice not to listen.)

At every crucial turn, Darwin listened to the highest—that is, the kindest and most humane—voices of his time, and was usually publicly numbered among them. In 1865, just after the American Civil War, the British governor of Jamaica massacred several hundred "natives" in order to end what he imagined was an incipient rebellion. In England, indignant citizens formed a "Jamaica Committee," intending to have the governor tried for murder. John Stuart Mill was the man who chaired the committee and pushed the point, but Darwin and Huxley were both on the committee (as was the geologist Charles Lyell), and their evolutionary views were assumed to be the source of their indignation. (The *Pall*

Mall Gazette sneered: "It would be curious also [to] know how far Sir Charles Lyell's and Mr. Huxley's peculiar views on the development of species have influenced them in bestowing on the negro that sympathetic recognition which they are willing to extend even to the ape as 'a man and a brother.' ")

And (closer to our own dual preoccupations), in 1873, Darwin wrote to Colonel Higginson, the American writer and friend to Emily Dickinson, who had recorded his experiences leading a black Union regiment in the Civil War:

> My wife has just finished reading aloud your "Life with a Black Regiment," and you must allow me to thank you heartily for the very great pleasure which it has in many ways given us. I always thought well of the negroes, from the little which I have seen of them; and I have been delighted to have my vague impressions confirmed, and their character and mental powers so ably discussed. When you were here I did not know of the noble position which you had filled. I had formerly read about the black regiments, but failed to connect your name with your admirable undertaking.

The "admirable undertaking" was the creation and employment of black troops on an equal footing with white ones, a practice which, as we've seen, enraged the racist South to the point of massacre.

Bad men often think big thoughts. Darwin *might* have been a racist and still have been right; that residual racism would have to be extracted from his ideas on evolutionary biology. But, as a matter of fact, he wasn't. And the connection that existed in the mind of his time was that his theory, tending toward proving the oneness of creation, naturally tended to prove the equality of men. Racism, in any form that would have been familiar in his time or would be familiar in ours, had no place either in Darwin's life or in Darwin's logic. Modern racism rests on the simple premise that races exist, and then that some are smarter or higher or purer than others. It begins in the belief that kinds of men are as different as species, that the *volk* is the reality and that the idea of the individual is the mere product of years of weakening acculturation, and bourgeois sentiment. Darwin was not only passionately opposed to all these views, but provided the best weapons to prove them wrong: evolutionary theory is a long explanation of why only individuals have a real existence, while races and species, far from being fixed and authoritative, are just convenient temporary designations of populations whose only real rule is that they vary. (Of course, species and even, at times, races are things we can talk about sensibly for the moment; we can tell a bear from a panda, and Asians from Africans. But they don't have the "real existence in nature" they did before Darwin; they're part of history, not permanent natural order, and there's lots of variation within the groups.) Variation, not conformity, is the Darwinian rule. Darwin's great and repeated theme was not the short-term success of certain races, but the permanent nonexistence of any.

Darwin himself was released by the publication of *The Origin*— the great struggle was over, and he had won at least a serene space for himself in which to work. He rapidly went from garden duffer to grand old man. Yet he didn't entirely enjoy it. Darwin, though filled with bright ideas and keen arguments on almost every subject under the sun, hated to be placed in the position of a wise man or oracle even as he became one. He felt helpless in the face of the kind of universal questions great men get asked: What should we make of the future? Will the United States be the major power? At one moment after he became famous, a group of a hundred and fifty German naturalists sent him, as a weird keepsake, an album of signed photographs of themselves—one imagines them all, bespectacled and scowling and impressive. It was the kind of thing that wore Darwin out; "we have been rather overdone with Germans this week," his wife sighed on another, similar occasion. (These days, it's Americans.) When he wrote an autobiography, meant as a posthumous gift for his children, it was candid and affectionate but remote and a little formal. He was timid and easily embarrassed, shrinking from confrontation and violent statement while remaining simultaneously stubborn, opinionated, and convinced beyond reason that he was right and his way of life and views about it were the only sane ones that a man of common sense could hold.

Darwin's strategy was one of the greatest successes in the history of rhetoric, so much so that we are scarcely now aware that it was a strategy, and it immediately inserted him into the Victorian pantheon. His pose of open-mindedness and ostentatiously asserted country virtue made him, in his way, as unassailable as George Washington. Clean-shaven through his youth, he grew a proper set of whiskers as he began to go public, and was photographed by Julia Cameron, every bearded inch the sage.

Retreating into his garden, widely known to be ill, publishing as often about earthworms and orchids as about men and apes—the notion persists to this day that Darwin was a diffident and circumspect observer of animals, not a confident theorist of life. Darwin was humble and modest in exactly the way that Lieutenant Columbo is humble and modest. He knows from the beginning who the guilty party is, and what the truth is, and would rather let the bad guys hang themselves from arrogance and overconfidence while he walks around in his raincoat, scratching his head and saying, "Oh, yeah—just one more thing about that six-thousand-year-old earth, Reverend Snodgrass . . ." Darwin was a civil and courteous man, but he was also what is now polemically called a Darwinian fundamentalist. He knew that he was right, and that his being right meant that much else people wanted to believe was wrong. Design was just chance plus time, greed not a sin from the devil but an inheritance from the monkeys. "Our descent, then, is the origin of our evil passions!!" he had written in his notebook back in that magical year of 1838. "The Devil under form of Baboon is our grandfather!" Under the beard and beneath the sage wrinkles, he never lost the inner confidence reflected in those words, nor the urge to provocation, and found ways of getting them both expressed in his books.

The discrepancy between the public and the private Darwin, the wide-eyed naturalist and the canny private politician, can make him sound like a bit of a phony, or at least like a shrewder operator than we want our saints to be: Janet Browne shows how carefully the Darwin-Huxley alliance took over the key positions in the London scientific societies of their day. Yet Darwin's rhetoric, coupled with Huxley's tactics, explains one of the most easily missed things about his revolution. Given that his was the most fundamental and successful challenge to dogma that had ever been launched—in a single generation, it caused intelligent people to accept claims about history and man's place in it that had been heretical for thousands of years—its reception was, as we've seen, remarkably peaceable. Of course, it inspired enormous controversy, but that controversy was far less battering than Darwin himself must have imagined. Victoria read him, Disraeli mocked him, the debates were held, and Darwin, the man who told the world that their forebears had been monkeys in trees with pointed ears, was almost offered a knighthood and buried in Westminster Abbey, as grand a figure as Tennyson or Browning.

But the real meat and juice of the post-*Origin* Darwin lies in the books he wrote after 1860, which, almost as much as that masterpiece, are wonders of observation, argument, and mischief.

He found new ways again and again not just to describe nature but also to *dramatize* nature. He oscillated between books on very finely drawn subjects—orchids and earthworms—and larger pop books on big subjects. In them all, he shows an immense and artful skill at distributing detail and delaying detonations, playing out the string and then pulling up the drawbridge.

Reading *The Descent of Man, and Selection in Relation to Sex* (1871), for instance, you feel an urge to draw analogies between his study of the way that birds' plumage and song affect their reproductive success and the way men dress up and show off in order to attract women—an urge so overwhelming that you practically have to bite your tongue to avoid it. Darwin bit his. (Generations have not so bitten, with predictable results.) Page after page goes by, in which the analogies to courtship, love, and flirtation are soberly avoided; when he quotes a French naturalist who uses just such larksome language, Darwin dutifully keeps it in the original French, as Gibbon kept the sexual escapades of the looser Romans in the original Latin.

But this turns out to be buildup, not letdown. After fourteen chapters of copious detail on the preening of the bronze-winged pigeon of Australia (which, "whilst standing before the female, lowers his head almost to the ground, spreads out and raises perpendicularly his tail, and half expands his wings") and the song of the European male bustard (which utters during breeding season "a peculiar sound resembling 'ock' "), the argument once again gets paid out:

> What then are we to conclude from these facts and considerations? Does the male parade his charms with so much pomp and rivalry for no purpose? Are we not justified in believing that the female exerts a choice, and that she receives the addresses of the male who pleases her most? It is not probable that she consciously

deliberates; but she is most excited or attracted by the most beautiful, or melodious, or gallant males. Nor need it be supposed that the female studies each stripe or spot of colour; that the peahen for instance, admires each detail in the gorgeous train of the peacock. . . . Nevertheless after hearing how carefully the male Argus pheasant displays his elegant primary wing feathers and erects his ocellated plumes in the right position for their full effect; or again how the male goldfinch alternately displays his gold-bespangled wings, we ought not to feel too sure that the female does not attend to each detail of beauty. We can judge, as already remarked, of choice being exerted, only from the analogy of our own minds, and the mental powers of birds, if reason be excluded, do not fundamentally differ from ours.

Having studiously avoided comparisons for hundreds of pages packed with ornithological detail, the entire book springs to, so to speak, wild life. Beauty and melody and gallantry, elegance and display, female choice—all are asserted to be as much a part of nature as egg laying. And so, at last, is a firm insistence: we are on a mental continuum with pheasants and peacocks. Analogy is avoided, and then the most unsettling analogy of all is grandly asserted, and without apology: they're us; we're them. This is Darwin's method: an apparently modest allegiance to mere fact gathering abruptly crystallizes in a whole worldview.

Darwin's ability to look pious while demolishing every piety can be seen at its best in what may be the single most explosive sentence in English, which appears in the last chapter of *The Descent of Man:* "We thus learn that man is descended from a hairy quadruped, furnished with a tail and pointed ears, probably arboreal in its habits, and an inhabitant of the Old World." Darwin does quietly lay the ground for the fireworks early in his book. His first chapter, on "rudiments," discusses in detail the many resemblances between human and animal anatomy. "It is notorious that man is constructed on the same general type or model as other mammals," he writes, and then expands on the point, detailing the resemblances at length, and then arriving at last at the observation, which he credits to "the celebrated sculptor, Mr. Woolner," that there is a "little blunt point" in the human ear, "projecting from the inwardly folded margin, or helix." By a sequence of oblique deductions about the ears of monkeys observed in the zoo, Darwin concludes that there are "vestiges of the tips of formerly erect and pointed ears" which occasionally reappear in man.

But though the fuse is quietly lit, the explosion still surprises. We can be startled by its boldness today; we know what its effect was in 1871. Yet how beautifully it is situated within the book, as, after that first chapter, we lose the plot in hundreds of detailed pages on sexual selection, on peacocks' tails and mammals' tusks, by which point it is presented not as a thesis to be demonstrated (although that was exactly what it was) but as a conclusion forced inexorably on the unwilling author. And then the sly choice of words—the "*hairy* quadruped" (unnecessary for the point but necessary to make the image maximally disturbing) and the dynamite of that tail and those "pointed ears," with their specific invocation of the diabolical, and the use of the domestic "furnished." There are a thousand ways the sentence could have been written in order to minimize its damage to belief; for example, "Those primates closest in organization and structure to man may have had their early origins among arboreal quadrupeds native to the Old World." But, a decade after *The Origin,* he writes instead the mortar sentence, the one that makes the minimal noise coming in and does the maximum damage on arrival. *There's* your grandfather: in a tree on all fours, his ears sticking straight up and his tail swinging through the branches.

The aftershocks of his early work continued, inflected by the triumph of his big idea. With the onset of evolutionary theory, the argument over Darwin's early theory about coral reefs at first sank away into the background—until Alexander Agassiz revived it. Alexander's father, Louis, was the Swiss-born maker of American natural history, and he became Darwin's first great creationist opponent. Dogmatic, difficult, and determined, he dominated American natural history until the spread of Darwin's ideas left him high and dry and even, eventually, a figure of ridicule. His son, a smart and decent man, recognized that his father had been both arrogant and wrong—he greatly admired Darwin, at first—and that evolutionary theory was probably sound. But he became increasingly impatient with the coral-reef theory, and hurt, too, by the Darwinian overkill aimed at his father.

Darwin, while pretending to treat his father with deferential respect, wrote letters to friends that mocked the old man's pretensions, urged on his opponents, and delighted at his eventual downfall. In one letter, Darwin thanked Charles Lyell for sending him a pamphlet on Amazonian geology by Louis Agassiz; "I was very glad to read it, though chiefly as a psychological curiosity," he wrote. "What a splendid imagination Agassiz has. . . . It is wonderful that he should have written such wild nonsense." (When Darwin's memoir was published after his death, the younger Agassiz was dismayed by its contents. "I was surprised . . . to see the element of . . . [Darwin] wishing his cause . . . brought out so prominently," Alexander wrote to a marine-biologist friend. "The one thing always claimed by Darwin's friends . . . had been his absolute impartiality to his own case.")

Alexander Agassiz spent his final decades trying to demonstrate the truth of his father's own theory of coral-reef formation: that coral reefs are formed when the millions of minuscule coelenterate skeletons pile up in vast mountains of shells; those, not

Darwin's sunken mountains, were what provided coral with its shallow-water platform. He traveled endlessly, and spent millions of dollars, in an effort to prove this inductively until, to his own satisfaction, he thought he had.

In the end, Darwin turned out to be right about that, too. After World War II, almost a century after he had come up with the subsidence theory, engineers finally had drills hard enough to bore past layers of coral and find out what lay beneath. It was rock, not organic matter; those volcanoes really had sunk, another account of life on earth changing and producing gloriously complicated and beautiful things through contingency and chance.

Yet for all his triumphs, and his deep-in-the-bone English sureness and even arrogance, he never appeared in public playing in a prideful key. Everywhere in Darwin's late work, the radicalism of his points is half concealed by the calming expansiveness of his syntax. He is gentle but unyielding on the religious question. "I am aware that the assumed instinctive belief in God has been used by many persons as an argument for His existence," he writes toward the end of *The Descent*. "But this is a rash argument. . . . The idea of a universal and beneficent Creator of the universe does not seem to arise in the mind of man, until he has been elevated by long-continued culture." In short, belief in the divine is man-made, not God given. As Lyanda Haupt points out, Darwin called his book *The Descent of Man,* not *The Ascent,* denying his readers the solace of an upward arc. Believers search for a crumb of comfort or teleology in Darwin, but what looks promising always turns out to be poisoned.

He and Emma, agnostic and believer, man and wife, stayed together till the end, and showed no signs of strain or unhappiness. However much she had feared his publishing his heresies, when the day came, she found that her love was stronger than her faith—

or, rather, that her love *was* her faith. They continued on in their life at Down House, retreating, as long-married people will, particularly after most of the children were out of the house, into a kind of willed mutual dependency that had some of the aspects of an Eliotian marriage of equals, some of a Beckettian folie à deux.

The beautiful and touching thing is that once he had at last taken the decision to publish that he had delayed so long in part on her behalf, she seems never to have blamed him, or reproached him, or felt burdened by his now-public aid to "disbelief." Small signs of difference, tempered by courtesy, persisted between them. He wrote to Karl Marx's son-in-law, upon being asked to have a radically antireligious book dedicated to him, that

> I am a strong advocate for free thought on all subjects, yet it appears to me (whether rightly or wrongly) that direct arguments against christianity & theism produce hardly any effect on the public; & freedom of thought is best promoted by the gradual illumination of men's minds, which follows from the advance of science. It has, therefore, been always my object to avoid writing on religion, & I have confined myself to science. I may, however, have been unduly biassed by the pain which it would give some members of my family, if I aided in any way direct attacks on religion.

Emma, in turn, gently bowdlerized his autobiography for publication, removing the most aggressively agnostic bits.

But at some point in his last years, he came upon that letter that she had written so long ago, when he had first decided to "Marry—Marry—Marry," telling him how pained she would be by his defection to disbelief, and that she "would be most unhappy if I thought we did not belong to each other forever." He scribbled at the bottom: "When I am dead, know that many times, I have kissed & cryed over this." When he was dying at last, in 1882, he whispered to her on his deathbed, with no plan for an afterlife, "My love, my precious love."

In 1881, the year before his death, he published one last improbable "commercial" volume with John Murray: *On the Formation of Vegetable Mould, through the Action of Worms*. It must have seemed like a perverse gesture to the publisher—the kind of thing greeted around the office with a sigh and a memory of old days and greater sales. But it's quite a book. Darwin begins by devoting to worms the same meticulous, worrying attentiveness that he before had given to man and monkeys, with a record of one of the more winning experiments ever attempted by a great scientist:

> Worms do not posses any sense of hearing. They took not the least notice of the shrill notes from a metal whistle, which was repeatedly sounded near them; nor did they of the deepest and loudest tones of a bassoon. They were indifferent to shouts, if care was taken that the breath did not strike them. When placed on a table close to the keys of a piano, which was played as loudly as possible, they remained perfectly quiet. When the pots containing two worms which had remained quite indifferent to the sound of the piano were placed on this instrument, and the note C in the bass clef was struck, both retreated into their burrows. After a time they emerged, and when G above the line in the treble clef was struck, they again retreated.

It is said that the Darwin family participated in this earthworm quartet, including Darwin's new grandson, who played the whistle. Darwin goes on to consider the earthworm's mind:

Mental Qualities—There is little to be said on this head. We have seen that worms are timid. It may be doubted whether they suffer as much pain when injured as they seem to express by their contortions. Judging by their eagerness for certain kinds of food, they must enjoy the pleasure of eating. Their sexual passion is strong enough to overcome for a time their dread of light. They perhaps have a trace of social feeling, for they are not disturbed by crawling over each other's bodies, and they sometimes lie in contact. . . . Although worms are so remarkably deficient in the several sense-organs, this does not necessarily preclude intelligence, as we know from such cases as those of Laura Bridgman; and we have seen that when their attention is engaged, they neglect impressions to which they would otherwise have attended; and attention indicates the presence of a mind of some kind. . . .

. . . Some degree of intelligence appears . . . to be exhibited in this work—a result that has surprised me more than anything else in regard to worms.

(Laura Bridgman, by the way, was blind and deaf-mute yet mastered language, a proto–Helen Keller.) As usual with Darwin, the slow crawl of fact is building toward a big blade of point. "Worms have played a more important part in the history of the world than most persons would at first suppose," he writes, and then explains:

When we behold a wide, turf-covered expanse, we should remember that its smoothness, on which so much of its beauty depends, is mainly due to all the inequalities having been slowly levelled by worms. It is a marvellous reflection that the whole of the superficial mould over any such expanse has passed, and will again pass through the bodies of worms. The plough is one of the most ancient and most valuable of man's inventions; but long before he existed the land was in fact regularly ploughed, and still continues to be thus ploughed by earth-worms. It may be doubted whether there are many other animals which have played so important a part in the history of the world, as have these lowly organised creatures.

He then clinches, and ends, with a crucial and suggestive point: "Some other animals, however, still more lowly organised, namely corals, have done far more conspicuous work in having constructed innumerable reefs and islands in the great oceans; but these are almost confined to the tropical zones." Small makes big; earthworms look like dinosaurs compared with coral-reef creatures, and look what they do!

Darwin's expansive consciousness—his empathy with the earthworm, no big deal but crucial to the history of the world—always narrows to a repeated rapier point: slow and steady wins the race and makes the races; we are allowed only a tiny glimpse, in our hummingbird lives, of what duration and endurance and repetition can actually achieve. We have a moral and scientific duty to seek out those places—coral reefs and earthworm-plowed fields as well as fossil pits and mussel-moved mountains—where we can get at least a sense of how an earthworm can do a farmer's work, if you give him time.

All of Darwin's virtues as a writer are in place in this improbable best seller (which it became, shocking the publisher as it pleased the readers). *The Origin* and *The Descent of Man* are more obviously great books, masterpieces of the human spirit. But if I had to pick one book to sum up what was great and rich in Charles Darwin, and in Victorian science and the Victorian mind more generally—a book to place alongside *Middlemarch* and *Phineas Finn* and *Through the Looking Glass* and *Great Expecta-*

tions—it might well be *On the Formation of Vegetable Mould, through the Action of Worms.* Limitless patience for measurement (the same virtue we see at similarly comic length in Ruskin's *Stones of Venice*), an ingenuous interest in the world in all its aspects, a desire to order many things in one picture, a faith that the small will reveal the large. And a gift for storytelling: Darwin makes the first person address never feel odd or strange in this scientific text, because we understand that the author is in a personal relation with his subject, probing, testing, sympathizing, playing the bassoon while the earthworms listen and striking the piano while they cower, and trying in every way to see who they are and where they came from and what they're like—not where they stand in the great chain of being beneath us, but where they belong in the great web of being that surrounds us, and includes us.

And then the great Darwinian themes are struck one last time, in a poignant, comic key: time itself, and slow modification, earthworms burrowing and the earth altering. Darwin was not especially preoccupied by the problems that move some Darwinians today: he readily saw through the puzzle of ostensibly intelligent design. (An eye that works well evolved from eyes that worked less well.) And, because he didn't know about genes, the great hole at the center of his argument—how did inheritance happen?—was one he never solved. But he was obsessed with the problem of time: How old is the earth? Has there been enough time for evolution to happen? As men dig up the bones that show just how ancient life really is, what lessons can you learn? How can you imagine time in a way that seems to make sense of our own lives and emotions?

For that, far more than God and man, is what Darwin is really always returning to: life and time, life and time, and their complements, death and sex, and how they make the history of life. In Darwin's work, from *The "Beagle"* to the earthworm, time moves at two speeds: there is the vast abyss of time in which generations change and animals mutate and evolve, and then there is the gnat's-breath, hummingbird-heart time of creaturely existence, where our children are born and grow and, sometimes, die before us. The space between the tiny but heartfelt time of human life and the limitless time of Nature became Darwin's implicit subject, running from The "Beagle" to The Origin. Religion had always reconciled quick time and deep time by pretending that the one was in some way a prelude to the other—a prelude or a prologue or a trial or a treatment. Artists of the Romantic period, in an increasingly secularized age, thought that through some vague kind of transcendence they could bridge the gap. They couldn't. Nothing could. The tragedy of life is not that there is no God but that the generations through which it progresses are too tiny to count very much. There isn't a special providence in the fall of a sparrow, but try telling that to the sparrows. The human challenge that Darwin felt, and that his work still presents, is to see both times truly—not to attempt to humanize deep time, or to dismiss quick time, but to make enough of both without overlooking either.

Writers of varying degrees of skill have recently tried to vindicate Darwin for students of literature by emphasizing his modest "sense of wonder," the almost mystical awe at the sheer existence of life in the universe. Darwin disenchanted believers in heaven, but he reenchanted lovers of earth. The philosophical George Levine, for instance, proposes an "enchanted secularity" to be deduced from Darwin: because Darwin robbed mankind of place and purpose, he gave us a chance to love and revere nature "precisely in its refusal to be like us."

These philosophical Darwinites are always on the side of the angels. But sometimes they are on the side of the angels when they ought to be on the side of the apes. If Darwin offers us a disenchanted universe—a universe drained of magic and of meaning—what would it be like to live in an enchanted one? Religious faith, after all, often sees itself as bedeviled and beleaguered even when it reigns more or less unchallenged. Conversely, the soulless materialism of the Darwinian universe can be a comfort: one wishes that a Darwinian could have been by Dr. Johnson's deathbed as he sank into a desperate fear of eternal damnation for having lusted after actresses in his youth. He would have found solace in the idea that there was nothing out there save oblivion, and that the world would remember the things that he had said on earth.

Although we can deduce from Darwin a new doctrine of "enchanted secularism"—or, indeed, Edward O. Wilson's proposal of a "scientific humanism"—we don't need to add to him to love what he says about life. For Darwinism has never been a threat to humanism; it *is* humanism, in flight. By humanism, we can mean two things. One is that man is the measure of all things; the other, that all things can be measured by man. The first view, essentially religious in origin, inspired Renaissance painting and the Sistine ceiling and Vitruvian proportions. The second view— that what makes people uniquely interesting is their capacity for gauging their environment and changing it, that the more we measure, the more accurately we see what things are actually like—has been what we have meant by humanism since the scientific revolution of the seventeenth century, and Darwin is one of its greatest exponents and examples.

Reading Darwin as a natural novelist shows us a Darwin as complex as good writers should be. He ended as a skeptical materialist who had proved that the forms of life were shaped by history, not by a supervising mind. But reading him also shows us that no emotion we would fear losing is lost in the transformation. The hardest Darwinian view of all is still roomy enough for ordinary love to breathe in.

Darwin was a Darwinian fundamentalist. But he was not a Darwinian absolutist. He knew that what feels to us like soul or spirit—the flash of understanding at an infant's smile or grief at a child's death—can never be argued away. He thought that he had found the secret of life. But he knew that nothing could solve the problems of living. That takes all the time we have.

AGES & ANGELS

Subsequent editions of the first Epistle [of the *Essay on Man*] exhibited two memorable corrections. At first, the poet and his friend "Expatiate freely o'er this scene of man, A mighty maze *of walks without a plan*." For which he wrote afterwards "A mighty maze, *but not without a plan*": for, if there were no plan, it was in vain to describe or to trace the maze.

—Samuel Johnson, "Life of Pope"

"Yes!" said the fairy, solemnly, half to herself, as she closed the wonderful book. "Folks say now that I can make beasts into men, by circumstance, and selection, and competition, and so forth. Well, perhaps they are right; and perhaps, again, they are wrong. That is one of the seven things which I am forbidden to tell, till the coming of the Cocq-cigrues; and, at all events, it is no concern of theirs. Whatever their ancestors were, men they are; and I advise them to behave as such, and act accordingly."

—Charles Kingsley, *The Water-Babies*

Science—scientific reasoning—seems to me an instrument that will lag far, far behind. For look here, the earth has been thought to be flat. It was true, so it still is today, for instance, between Paris and Asnières. Which however does not prevent science from proving that the earth is principally round. Which no one contradicts nowadays.

But notwithstanding this they persist nowadays in believing that life is flat and runs from birth to death. However, life too is probably round, and very superior in expanse and capacity to the hemisphere we know at present.

—Vincent van Gogh, June 1888

Tides and splashes, angels and ages—heretical thoughts fill one's head at the end of a long walk through the past. Would the tides of history and ideas *really* have changed had neither man ever made a splash? Can we imagine modern life, and liberal civilization, just as well without either man?

Darwinism, after all, might have been achieved without Darwin, just as the North would most probably have won the Civil War, and slavery would have ended around the same time, without Lincoln. Alfred Wallace had the idea of natural selection—but, as he knew perfectly well, he was not competent to write a book of the scale or persuasiveness of *The Origin*. He had none of the larger arguments, none of the crushing waves of evidence, none of the deeply meditated grasp of the difficulties. But weren't there other naturalists in touch with the larger evidence, and wasn't Huxley always there to shape the evidence into argument? Yes. Had it emerged that way, though, evolution by natural selection would have appeared only as a footnote, slowly infiltrating the general consciousness, exactly as Mendel's genetics did later. Without Darwin's craftily humble eloquence and exhaustive, encyclopedic evidence, evolutionary biology would never have carried the day so quickly. (And it did. Although the details of Darwin's views on adaptation and natural selection were not universally accepted until the neo-Darwinian synthesis of the 1940s, by the end of the nineteenth century his core point was already in place: in 1858, few people publicly believed that species were mutable; by 1900, essentially everyone did. The arguments, loud ones, were all about what it meant, and exactly how it happened, not whether it had.)

Character counts; eloquence illuminates. A useful comparison is to Charles's good friend Charles Babbage, who came as close to solving the problem of mechanical computation as Darwin did to solving the problem of the origin of species. Babbage's "difference engines," the first programmable computers, could have ushered in a fin de siècle cybernetic revolution. But Babbage was, as Darwin tells us, "a disappointed and discontented man; and his expression was often or generally morose. . . . One day he told me that he had invented a plan by which all fires could be effectively stopped, but added,—'I shan't publish it—damn them all, let all their houses be burnt.' " (Babbage also once remarked, "There is only one thing which I hate more than piety, and that is patriotism.") Darwin observed, correctly, that Babbage's "bark was much worse than his bite," but his bark caused him to be seen, as the English say, as barking—nuts. And so the first computers would be left unfinished and largely unknown. Had Babbage been a writer and advocate as gifted as Darwin, and Darwin as much a maverick and a pill as Babbage, we might have had steam-driven art nouveau–styled personal computers in the early twentieth century, while evolutionary biology would have been left a murky mess until after the Second World War.

Without Darwin, no Darwinism—but might it perhaps, just perhaps, have been just as well? Had Darwinism not been Darwinism, it might have kicked up less ideological dust, some of which is surely noxious. Exasperated by the way specious arguments over evolution are sustained in the guise of personal arguments over Darwin, a few professional biologists, like Olivia Judson, have even undertaken to have the very word *Darwinism* replaced in discussion of his legacy. Darwinism is just what Darwin happened to say, they point out, while evolutionary biology is the science that grew out of it. As things stand, the argument goes, anti-evolutionists can obsess about Darwin's agnosticism, or his relationship to eugenics, as though these things had any meaning or impact on what goes on in biology today. The name, they argue, implies an undue cult relation between the maker and his theory. There is no more point in calling evolutionary biology "Darwinism" than in calling the theory of gravity "Newtonism" or that of relativity "Einsteinism." Evolutionary biologists are rightly amused, or offended, when this or that pundit claims to "have issues" with Darwinian thinking, or to have found a hole in Darwinian logic. After all, would one publish the news that a pundit isn't satisfied with the theory of gravity, or doubts that the earth goes round the sun? Evolution is by now as well established by argument and evidence and reproducible experiment as any truth of physics or cosmology, as well established a theory as any in the history of science. (Which means, of course, that it continues to be altered and amended. That's why they call it science, and a theory.)

Understandable professional exasperation aside, a change of name would be a mistake. Though evolutionary biology does exist today independent of, even far removed from, Darwin's personal example, Darwinism is more than a set of claims; it is an entire epoch in human thought and feeling. His habits of mind—fairness, popular address, and the annealing of courage with tact—are worth revering even if scientists abandon or revise half of his tenets. The power of his example—an appetite for seeing joined to a capacity for seeing past, a love of observation enabling a gift for rigorous inference—would be right even if his ideas were wrong. It was Darwin's inductive eloquence that made evolutionary biology happen in the admirable way that it did—the patient, exhaustive piling up of instances from botany, evidence from geology, facts of embryology, all hard-won things that he had seen for himself—along with the ability to give the pile a significant shape. Someone else *might* have done all that. But no one else did.

Great books of science, like all great books, are worth reading not just for what they add to objective knowledge; they are worth reading because they advance our liberal education. Just as we don't read Dante for a sneak peek at the afterlife or because we expect someday to be confronted with a diabolical architecture of circles within circles and punishments suited to our sins, we don't read Darwin because what he says is what scientists now believe—much of it isn't. We read him because a book of eloquent argument and well-ordered evidence, assembled with such modest yet personal passion, reminds us of the powers of the human mind to bring light to darkness, make a clearing in the wood of confusion. As Dr. Johnson said about the man who could ride on three horses at once, it matters because it shows what people are capable of doing if they try.

Even Darwin's way of being wrong was the right way of being wrong. As Huxley wrote immediately after the publication of *The Origin:* "Twenty years hence naturalists may be in a position to say whether this is, or is not, the case; but in either event they will owe the author of *On the Origin of Species* an immense debt of gratitude. We should leave a very wrong impression on the reader's mind if we permitted him to suppose that the value of that work depends wholly on the ultimate justification of the theoretical views which it contains. On the contrary, if they were disproved to-morrow, the book would still be the best of its kind." The best of its kind because it asks the right questions in the right spirit, and enlarges the human mind by its very existence. It is not blind belief in Darwin's view of nature but our love for what he did to the blind nature of belief that makes biology, and us, Darwinist. By honoring Darwin, we aren't idolizing him. Just the opposite, really. If Darwinism *were* like a religion, then the Darwinism practiced now would be a sect, unlike the original and at war with the first faith, Sufis to the old sect's Sunnis. We can say that bits of it are right, and bits of it look wrong, and lots of bits aren't pinned down yet. Anomalies at the edges are not the same as heresies on the horizon.

It is, in a way, a tribute to Lincoln's greatness that we can even mention the two men together: Lincoln is, after all, a provincial figure, one man in one country, an actor largely ex officio, while Darwin is an epoch maker. We lived in an American century, but we live in a Darwinian world. Certainly it's possible that, had Lincoln been assassinated in Maryland on his way to the presidency—rather than saved by Pinkerton—a Secretary Seward working through a feeble President Hamlin might have done as well, or even better. He might have been less impressed by a dress-up general like McClellan and, though he wouldn't have gone to Grant, might well have turned to *someone* good, and been less patient with the obvious screwups. For that matter, had common cause been made with the rest of North America, as Darwin suggested, cooler and wiser heads might have prevailed sooner, slavery might have ended, and a Greater North America today might be a flourishing nation, albeit more like Australia (big, less populated, a little bit inclined to cringe across the ocean).

Nor are Lincoln's claims of "national unity," of "Union," so obviously irresistible—although it helps to have lived outside America to see this. In Canada, for instance, the issue of the secession of Quebec has risen, again and again, with the general conclusion that if the people, even a small majority of the people, of Quebec decide that they want to have their own country, Canada will be obliged to let them go. It is a fraught issue, and a demand for "clarity" has been added to it, in recognition of the reality that the verdict of a single "snapshot" moment hardly seems enough to doom a country. But the principle of potential separation is held to because of the understanding that the alternative is armed violence. For that matter, we endure, and even encourage, the breakup of other countries—the old Yugoslavia, Czechoslovakia—into smaller parts, again guided by the perceived good of self-determination and also the prudential judgment that the alternative would be civil war.

Well, civil war was the alternative in America, too, and Lincoln chose it. We see the choice as both morally right and historically successful, but we see it as morally right in part because it *was* historically successful. Harry Truman said, with artless honesty, that he liked Lincoln best of all the presidents because he allowed Truman to be important, but it isn't always clear to the majority of the earth's population that the American rise to global dominance resulting from the preservation of the Union has necessarily been a good thing. More profoundly, there is something dangerous about the equation of military success and moral right; the argument favoring violence for the sake of an ideal can make us idealize violence, and gets even liberal-minded people, who ought to know better, to forget what the actual costs of war are.

Or we might ask what would have happened if Lincoln had not been assassinated right after the war's end. Samuel Eliot Morison began a chapter in his synoptic history of America by calling down a thousand curses on the head of John Wilkes Booth, on the grounds that a living Lincoln would have eased the pains of Reconstruction. The trouble with this is that the pains of Reconstruction were not those of white people who needed a more sympathetic overseer but those of blacks who were promised freedom and then denied it by force. It is hard even for a Lincoln idolater to believe that Lincoln would not have put the demands of the old ruling class for more power over those of a helpless dark-skinned people for mere land and liberty. His taste for the "grease," his genuine appetite for conciliation, might very well have pressed Lincoln to make more concessions sooner to the returning rulers. It's possible, and nice to imagine, that Lincoln's stature and intelligence would have led him to find a way to enfranchise blacks without infuriating whites, but, given how hard it was to do in our own time, it doesn't seem too likely. The end of slavery had been at the center of his imagination for all his adult life; the integration of blacks had not. The only fair postwar peace would have been a hard peace, sustained by the army; a comparable peace has been possible in South Africa, for instance, only by the irresistible force of numbers. It's just as possible to imagine Lincoln floundering in peace as he had sailed straight in war, and ending up with another version of the same ugly mess that his successors got, eventually fleeing to Europe and the Holy Land and his memoirs, growing old with a potent but mixed reputation—not unlike that of his hero Jefferson, in a way. (When John F. Kennedy met Pandit Nehru, now no longer the philosopher-prophet of Indian independence but a tired and fretful old man, he remarked, with great savvy, to John Kenneth Galbraith that Nehru sadly put him in mind of what Lincoln might have been like had our nation-maker lived a quarter century past *his* triumph.) His death has dramatic point (if we can, as we shouldn't, overlook the mind-crushing grief it caused his wife) and inevitability—but it also locked his reputation in place as a prophet and poet, whereas his continued life might have left him remembered merely as a president.

Yet in another way it was an even bigger war, with bigger meanings, than Americans can quite see. We may overrate Lincoln's personal genius a little—as we eulogize, over and over, his faith, his speech, his shrewdness, and even his sadness—but we may also in an odd way underrate his accomplishment. We tend to overpraise the originality of his political procedures—*every* statesman in England and France brought his rivals into his cabinet. Yet we may still overlook the consequences of his cause. In England, John Stuart Mill, who never visited America or much wanted to, still followed the Civil War and Lincoln's acts with the sense that the war was "full of the most important consequences to humanity, stretching into the remotest future," and even that "the whole futurity of mankind" depended on it. What was at stake in this war for Mill was not only the end of slavery but the survival of liberal democracy itself, and the test of its survival was whether it could enforce its own laws against a morally deranged minority who didn't like them (the law that held that one man rather than another was the elected president or, more locally, that a fort belonged to the government that had built it). Mill, recognizing the tension between his belief in the right of self-determination and his opposition to the South, wrote that "secession may be laudable . . . but it may also be an enormous crime." In contemporary terms, Lincoln's success had the worldwide effect that Boris Yeltsin's might have had had he somehow been able to keep the Russian empire united while installing a functioning, law-bound democracy. Our own post-1989 hopes for liberalism as both a light and a lance, a humane creed capable of self-defense, would have risen immeasurably had Yeltsin only done that. Lincoln's success was of that kind, and of that scale.

After it was over, a new birth of freedom did take place. Ironically, the renaissance was in some ways less visible in America itself, where what has been fairly called the reenslavement of blacks took place under the rule of terror, and a plutocracy emerged in the North, than it was elsewhere. In England, the victory of the North helped pave the way for the Reform Bill of 1867 and engaged the English working classes in what Gladstone rightly called the "magnificent moral spectacle" of the fight against slavery in defiance of their own economic interest in the cotton trade; in France, the victory helped give confidence and a sense of purpose to the establishment of the Third Republic. The Statue of Liberty, though it has been incorporated into our history of immigration, stands in New York Harbor as a testament from one free country to another that liberty, after two thousand years, really does light the harbor. When we look at it, we should see our grandparents arriving. But we should think of Lincoln, too.

Lincoln and Darwin are both emblematic figures in the spread of bourgeois liberal democracy, and the central role for science that goes with it. They stand for those free and freely inquiring societies in their gift of eloquence, in their insistent need to persuade and convince, argue and substantiate, talk and justify. They remind us that literary style, eloquence, isn't an ornament or frosting on an achievement created by other means; it is part of that achievement. Lincoln and Darwin were not otherwise great figures who happened to be great writers; we pick them out among their contemporaries because they wrote so well, and they wrote so well because they saw so clearly, and they saw so clearly because they cleared their minds of the cant of their day and used the craft of legal and scientific reasoning to let themselves start fresh. Just as Lincoln used the narrow language of the law to arrive at a voice of liberalism still resonant and convincing today, Darwin used the still more narrow language of natural observation—of close amateur looking—to change our ideas of life and time and history. Darwin is most fully himself, most alive, in the volumes of narrow observational science that he published regularly in between his speculative books. The end of his life's work, which seems to some a descent, a dying fall—those worms and that vegetable mold—seemed nothing of the kind to him. Nor should it to us. It's the last Darwinian statement: truth comes from close scrutiny of the way things are, with the mind demanding every moment to know how the hell they got that way. The tininess is the point. In the same way, the legalistic side of Lincoln, the devotion to legal technicality so disconcertingly evident in the Emancipation Proclamation, or the buildup of his great Cooper Union speech, is inseparable from the celebrated soaring rhetorical Lincoln who saw the point of the thing: that no nation can be free and enslaved at once.

Induction and argument are the probity of liberal thought. Facts matter, logic counts, describing the stamen of the orchid exactly is worth six volumes on the metaphysics of being. The truth matters to the progress of a free nation—but it matters just as much that the truth be accepted. In an open society, new truths need to be told, and new truths need to be *heard*. It was Darwin's inductive eloquence that allowed science to rewrite the history of life; it was Lincoln's rational passion that ended the long horror of slavery, and began the adventure of democracy as a dominant, not a Utopian, way of life. Lincoln showed, to a degree that we no longer appreciate, that democratic politics are compatible with a society's long-term survival—or, to put it bluntly, with military victory, with winning armies; he showed that democracy can survive the use of force to preserve it. Darwin showed that scientific reasoning can explain not only the life of matter but the matter of life—it can come up with a plausible theory of the history of life on this planet, which until then had seemed as mysterious as the nature of time or consciousness seems to us now.

And this rootedness in reasoning explains why of all explanations of life, evolutionary theory is not remotely like a religion. There is no resemblance between evolutionary biology, even if we call it Darwinism, and a religion. (And it is the devil's work to say it is!) The theory of evolution by natural selection is an argument: all its points are open, its claims clear, many of its possible refutations self-evident. (Find the fossilized body of a Pekingese lapdog in the Pleistocene, and we all start over.) It deserves the respect we give to any wonderful and winning argument, the same respect that we give to the argument of the Declaration of Independence, or the Gettysburg Address. But it isn't a dogma, and the claim that it is is made only by those who want to protect their own faiths from criticism by pretending that all strong ideas can only take the form of faiths.

Darwin proudly called his idea of evolution by natural selection a "theory," which was not always the way that scientists talked about their ideas in the nineteenth century. In those 1838 notes on Maculloh's "Proofs of God," he refers twice on a single page to "my theory" in opposition to Maculloh's natural theology. The invocation of theory has something modest about it, but it is also "massive," as the kids say now; theology was to be countered by theories, which are tentative, open-ended, and unsure but also explain things that were otherwise mystifying, and are always empirical—open to probing and testing and changing. Theories, as the psychologists Alison Gopnik and Andy Meltzoff have pointed out, are in many ways the ground and basis of our humanity: it is in the child's ability to make theories, test them from experience, and then make new and better ones, that intelligence emerges; and it is, by the same argument, in the perversion of theory into dogma that intelligence becomes enslaved. A child who can't make new theories is a disabled child. Darwin's elevation of the dignity of theory is part of his elevation of the dignity of man, defined in a new way: not as a being who knows from birth, or is told from on high, but as one who asks and learns and asks again.

Yet Darwin and Lincoln both saw something more, and darker, than the strength of good speech and open-ended ideas. They learned that death was all around and all-powerful. They learned it firsthand through the deaths of those they loved, and they learned it just as cruelly, if at a greater distance, from those who died in war or in the struggle for existence. Lincoln's compassion for the soldiers he knew he had led to an early death was real and immediate; it's one of the things that make us admire him. But Darwin's compassion for even the simple creatures who died horribly in nature was real, too; the caterpillar eaten away from inside by the ichneumon wasp's larvae genuinely made him doubt that any good deity could oversee the world. Death was the one fact whose force could not be argued out, only accepted. It couldn't be explained persuasively in terms of due process. It couldn't be brought down to earth by the most painstaking of descriptions. It called them both to seek some form of transcendence, some meaning beyond the human cycle of breathing and eating and dying, even while resisting the supernatural meanings of faith.

Their constant sense of the presence of death helps explain

why they both came to a new, almost mystical sense of the power of *time*—time the explanatory force, the justifying force that gives meaning to life by asking us to think in the very long term. Unable to see life "vertically," in terms of the verdict of heaven, they came to see it "horizontally," in terms of the judgment of time. Deaths at Cold Harbor or in the struggle for existence made some sort of sense in history, beyond individual imagination but within human imagination.

Darwin and Lincoln were makers and witnesses of the great change that, for good or ill, marks modern times: the slow emergence from a culture of faith and fear to one of observation and argument, and from a belief in the judgment of divinity to a belief in the verdicts of history and time. First, the change from soul to mind as the engine of existence, and then from angels to ages as the overseers of life. For good or ill, that is what we mostly mean by "modernity," and by the special conditions of modern times. Just as Lincoln looking at history could seem to make sense of the horror of war, Darwin, considering the deep time of evolution, could give some shape to the senseless wedge of death. This emergence, of course, is still seen by many as a terrible descent: the loss of the certainty of a single set of sure values. Yet their pain and problem is ours. Our beliefs are still likely to be touched by either Lincoln's agonized intuitive spirituality, his private religion, or by Darwin's calm domestic stoicism, his quiet doubt.

This faith in deep time gave each of them a different, and modern, spiritual turn. The American begins in aggressive freethinking and atheism so severe that it has been largely read out of the record and crosses, through the Civil War, toward some kind of private belief in providential fate and destiny, in many ways Jewish, or at least Old Testament, in tone. The Englishman begins in the inward-turning faith of the English church and clergy, for which his whole early life was designed, passes through quiet doubt, and ends in open atheism, which, with typical tact, he refers to only as uncertainty. He ended as a kind of classical Stoic. Lincoln became an American Job; Darwin, an English Marcus Aurelius. These two tracks cross in the sky above their time (and show, at crucial moments, a similar pang of acute doubt brought on by seeing children die too soon). Lincoln and Darwin take opposing trajectories toward two very near places, and rare is the modern person who hasn't, at some time or other, visited both: private mysticism touched by public secularism, shining inward faith in tension with scientific skepticism.

There is a curious double consciousness at large in liberal civilizations. On the one hand, they grant enormous importance to the individual and the individual's immediate connections—to family, garden, small group, the Little Women waiting. On the other, they have been shaped by mass death and a readiness for mass killing, by what Papa goes through in the Union army. (This imbalance may explain why we give murder such undue imaginative weight, why our most popular storytelling apparatus, nightly television, is so devoted to the lore and legends and compulsive retelling of individual homicides, even though their investigations are a vanishingly small percentage of what police officers really do.)

Lincoln and Darwin grasped this double truth—inhabited it, in fact. Modern liberal eloquence is rooted in fact, divided in feeling. It begins with a faith in what the eye sees and what the mind knows—and recognizes that the heart and soul seek more. In the mid-nineteenth century, when modernity was taking shape, most of the liberals and progressives were optimists; they believed that things were getting better, and would go on getting better. The poetic pessimists, Carlyle and Ruskin and Henry Adams, were all among the "reactionary" doubters. Evolution became joined to the idea of constant progress, government of the people to the idea of Manifest Destiny. For a long time in the twentieth century, with the eclipse of liberalism, the pessimists held more intellectual repute even as the optimists worked small wonders in the world. (This made for the awkward but important fact that reactionary politics and visionary art go together in the literary movement we call modernism.)

But as history changed and liberalism seemed, at the end of the twentieth century, with all its flaws and faults, not just admirable but for a moment at least victorious, the old evident banality intruded. We again need a sense of how we can reconcile it with the darker truths we know about the world, and which Darwin and Lincoln understood already. In their lifetimes, they took the fatuous and optimistic liberalism of triumphal democracy and ever-improving nature and improvised toward a fatalistic but far from despairing idea of Providence and the workings of time. All their angels are ages, and the ages held out a distant halo of angels. They found a way to sustain the necessary values of the Enlightenment in the face of pessimistic truths about the universe and political conduct. Persuasion wouldn't be enough in human affairs; war would be necessary. Nature was not benevolent, nor always tending to improve, but blindly cut a wedge of death through the innocent. But it was still possible to measure and speak and believe in the possibility of broader knowledge and a better world. There may be no plan, but we can still describe the maze; describing the maze is, in fact, the first step in getting out of it. Lincoln, as Garry Wills has shown us, revived the crucial Enlightenment document, the Declaration of Independence, and made it part of the war. Darwin gave his grandfathers' labile universe a mechanism and an explanation; he put the history of life on the same law-bound basis as the history of the universe. Evolution wasn't an impulse in each creature that we could only submit to; it was a cumulative law of the natural world that we could see. Darwin was a sort of Stoic, and Lincoln a "suffering man," but neither was merely resigned. Both gave liberalism a tragic consciousness without robbing it of a hopeful view.

In our optimism over their rhetoric, might we be missing an appropriate pessimism about their success? After all, slow, carefully argued evidentiary-minded speech sure doesn't *seem* like a winning ticket in modern life. And it isn't always, or perhaps even often. Alas—and that nineteenth-century rhetorical *alas* covers a genuine world of grief and pain—it's true that both men, and their ideas, for all they won, were also losers. Within a year of Lincoln's death, the great idea of Reconstruction was gone, and the resubjugation of black Americans, with slaves turned into serfs, was begun through terror, not to end until well into the next century. Lincoln stands out in his time because there is only one of him, one statesman with his moral vision. Darwin, for his part, planted the seeds of a natural universalism in the mind of the world, but nationalism and racism would turn out to be much stronger—so much stronger that Darwinism itself would be abused in the cause. That we remember them well doesn't mean they won. They may be icons, but icons still inspire prayers for lost causes.

There is, still, a real asymmetry in how they are remembered. Aside from a few loud doubters, Lincoln has been resettled in a cocoon of righteousness even as his real accomplishments have not always been well understood. Darwin, on the other hand, though even his smaller ideas have been vindicated over time, has been under increasing assault in the last few years, at least in America, from the conservative and fundamentalist right wing.

Traditionally, it was leftists, and Marxists in particular, who, despite the allegiance of Marx to its master, were the most hostile to Darwinism. They were passionately opposed to it, or just ignorant of it, for a simple reason: it seemed to downplay the control of economic life over human minds, saying that biology was strong, and free of social causes; it also seemed to posit a system of competition that, as we've seen, very superficially resembles free market capitalism. This double dubiousness led ultimately to the catastrophe of Lysenkoism, the doctrine that acquired characteristics can be inherited, which became dogma under Stalin, helping to stall Russian genetics and starve Russia. (Even today, many leftist lives of Darwin are written under a sign of extreme suspicion that he was merely serving capitalist masters by saying that creatures struggled in nature to survive, even though the analogy of nature and the market was not his own, nor implied by his work.)

Why, then, has the hostility shifted across the political spectrum? The philosopher Philip Kitcher provides part of the answer. Although in fact Darwinism was a late-arriving weapon in the Enlightenment's battle with superstition and religious fundamentalism—the work of doubt had already been done by the time *The Origin* appeared—most people are unaware of the Enlightenment critique in its earlier forms. We don't read or know Hume's criticism of miracles, or the nineteenth-century textual criticism of the Bible. (It is a fair guess that the overwhelming majority of Christians are unaware that the Gospel according to Mark did not originally include an account of the Resurrection.) But *everyone* takes biology. Everyone has to. And where it once offended leftists to be told that biology has an existence independent of class interests, it now offends conservatives to be told that biology has an existence independent of religious teaching, or the tradition of the West. And a certain callow triumphalism on the part of the community of popularizers—from which one should exempt even old opponents like Daniel Dennett and Stephen Jay Gould, both of whom recognized there's no explaining away emotion by reference to genes—encourages the upset.

The other, and deeper, reason for this anger is that the spread of pop Darwinism undermines the strength of the humanities—the tradition of the novel, and poetry and history as authority on human affairs—and of the authority of the people who have mastered those parts of culture to speak in an intimidating way on broad subjects. Edmund Wilson, Lionel Trilling, even T. S. Eliot—none of them really understood even the rudiments of evolutionary theory, yet no one, a scant two generations ago, questioned their right to speak on human affairs not just with wisdom but with authority, with a claim to have mastered the real fount of human wisdom about human life. More important even than our faith in God is allegiance to our Magi. The common reader is now more likely to go to Daniel Dennett or Richard Dawkins, to Steven Pinker or Steve Jones, for that kind of authority, translating academic expertise into moral exhortation. (And doing it in the same way: a bit of data, a touch of interpretation, and a lot of moral exhortation, as here.) The authority, for good or ill, has passed from the humanities proper to the sciences improper, from literary studies to popular science, and with that passage has come an inevitable and understandable reaction.

The truth is that Darwin implies no politics: one can be a passionate Darwinian and be of the far right, the right, the liberal center, the left, or even the far left; great Darwinians have been found all around the room.

A similar pluralism is possible in thinking about Darwinism's relationship to faith, despite the stormier and much louder arguments Darwinism provokes. Whether we ought to find the two unbridgeable, the truth is that we haven't. Darwinism has been the basis of biology for a century; meanwhile, fundamentalists remain fundamental, poets have gone on writing Christian poetry, and mystics have gone on doing mystical work. It's a good thing, actually, that we can't reconcile each of our beliefs with every other: the possibility of alteration is the healthiest aspect of our beliefs. Charles and Emma, Mr. and Mrs. Darwin, remained married and in love to the end.

Of course, it is possible to imagine a day when the forces of intolerance could overwhelm the habits of pluralism. But it hasn't happened, not yet, and not nearly, and the friends of pluralism do their cause no favors by trying to proclaim the day or pretend that it is nearer than it is. We live perfectly happily in a world with churches on the street corners and biology textbooks in the study. True liberalism begins with recognition of what is, and what is possible; so far, what is, is science and religion more or less cohabiting, more or less happily.

Perhaps the reason is this simple: religion has become for most an affirmation not of a certain understanding of history but of a way to live in the present; it is an expression of a social practice, of community ritual, and life seems sad without it. Anyone who has taken part in even the most debased or "secularized" forms of such rituals, the most godless seder or Unitarian kindergarten, knows that they are illuminating beyond all measure, and that life without them seems empty. A life without Christmas would be a life without stars. So if by religion we mean a faith in a supernatural being, an invisible man in the sky who makes absolute rules about human existence, punishing those who break them and then manifesting his existence from time to time in the Middle East for the purpose of issuing amendments, then, no, the truths of Darwinism are not compatible with religion. (That kind of God would have to have a very weird sense of humor, in any case, since life would be nothing but a very long shaggy-dog story, with us as the punch line, and we're not a big enough laugh for such a buildup—sixty million years of rocks and zombies and then an eye's blink of consciousness. You could get the joke told sooner with the same effect.) And of course if religion includes a doctrine of eternal damnation, then, as Darwin said, it is a damnable doctrine.

None of our serious religious thinkers has held such a view of God for a very long time. Ours has been an age of great theological speculation, sublime religious poetry, and profound personal revelation. Auden's *For the Time Being: A Christmas Oratorio*, Barth's theology—neither of them has the least quarrel with, or much interest in, evolutionary biology because that is not its subject any more than the history of life on earth is the subject of the Psalms. The subject of such works is evil and good, alienation and belonging. If by religion we mean belief in a force in the universe that nonetheless seems to shine inside us with a power that is inexplicable but real to all who witness it, and gives meaning and serenity to life, then, yes, religion is completely compatible with Darwinism, which is a claim about history, not about everything that is.

Or even if we mean by religion what most people have actually meant by it since the beginning of time—an encompassing practice of irrational rituals that can't be justified but only experienced, and give order and continuity to life—then, yes, of course, religion is compatible with Darwinism. The faith of George Herbert and Dr. Johnson, of Kierkegaard and W. H. Auden, has nothing to do with obeying the commandments of an invisible man in the sky who occasionally intervenes, and everything to do with confronting the chaotic reality of the cosmos to find serene order within it. In this sense the "epiphenomena" of religion—choral music, stained glass, Communion—are the thing itself.

It is odd how often people mention music when talking about faith; the existence of Handel's *Messiah* does not prove the existence of God, but the importance of Christianity is proved by the existence of the *Messiah*. To enter Chartres is to understand Catholicism. To secularize or "aestheticize" these things, thereby removing them from their dogmatic contexts, is to miss their meaning. The nativity of baby Jesus reminds us of the fragility of childhood, the wonder of renewal in birth, and the long shadow of a probably horrible death that hangs over every one of us, but it is more than a symbol, too. It's alive. Bach knew this, and we know it, too. The imaginative life, in which we make symbols and stories, is not a secondary existence of ours, but a primary one. It's how we're made to live. When we talk of souls and spirits, we are not talking nonsense any more than we are when we talk of love and courage and faith in some cause. Those ideas may not have a fixed material existence. But the most compelling things never do. The "fact-value" distinction that is so much a part of the modern philosophy of science—the rule that our values are not naturally determined but chosen—is *not* intended to belittle values; it is intended to diminish the tyranny of facts. It is a way of saying not that physical truths imply no morality but that morality is made irrespective of mere physical truths.

It might be true, for instance, that life is brutal and pointless, but we can choose to live as though it were otherwise. It might be true—there is absolutely no such evidence, but it might be true—that different ethnic groups, or sexes, have on average different innate aptitudes for math or science. We might decide to even things out, give some people extra help toward that end, or we might decide just to live with the disparity. (In any case, human populations are so large these days that the relatively tiny number of outliers who rise above the average is large enough to staff any university faculty you could want.) It certainly is true that the chances of anything we are doing now being remembered are vanishingly small, and the chances of the obliteration of life on the planet depressingly real—but we all choose to live as though what we are doing has meaning and purpose beyond the day and moment.

We make our values in the face of facts. And so the values are ours. We can't outsource them upward. The judgment that some act is right, rather than demonic, can only be our own. We can turn to faith for meaning, but not for morality. As everyone since Plato has recognized, our idea of good has to be independent of our idea of God, since a God who asks us to do evil is not one we can obey. The sacrifice of Isaac seems acceptable to us only because it didn't happen; it otherwise seems inscrutable, and we could not obey a God who would have let a father slay a son. Like Darwin, we would choose not to worship a God with bad rules and cruel intentions even if he existed. Only very simple people of faith any longer live by an unquestionable divine covenant. Even the most passionate faith is impossible without moral judgment made independent of it.

We can't look up to know how to act. But we can't look back, either. The notion that we can go back to the savanna, to our evolutionary past, for our moral principles is, at best, incoherent; if Darwin reveals anything, it is that no moment is privileged, no species perfected, nothing wrought but all nascent and nothing entirely achieved—sixty thousand years from now people might be referring to the ultimate moment in which human morality got fixed in the big cities of this era, when we were flourishing (which we certainly are doing, actually rather more successfully than our sparse savanna ancestors did). We can't outsource our lives, or our morality, either backward or upward.

Or anywhere else, except forward. We can't worship history any more than we can justify present pain for imaginary future pleasure. But we *can* make a better world. Pessimism is so much part of the mental equipment of modern people that to gainsay it is to seem unserious. But there is a difference between a tragic consciousness and pervasive pessimism. We don't know what Utopia would look like, but we do know the difference between bad and better. The world is better now than it was once, in the simplest and most important of ways. There are no slaves, at least not in America or England. The hold of fear and superstition has lessened. We know how men got here. Science has revealed many things, if not everything. Annie wouldn't die today. Neither would Willie. We might not be able to cure Tad, but we could help him. We have not yet found a way to avoid wars, but most people know that they have horrible consequences even when they are justified, and that we should begin them only when the life of the community we love and its values are obviously and overwhelmingly at risk. (Sometimes, they are. The pacifists are not always right. But the warmongers are almost always wrong.) There are fewer racists; more people are peace loving. Meanwhile, we can go on looking for the point of life—if there is one, other than to make the bad things better. That may have been the point all along. Between 1914 and 1945 the great reactions against the open society produced sixty million deaths in Europe, and it seemed natural, and right, for us to become pessimistic about modernity itself. To discard those doubts for a fatuous complacency is wrong. But what is most striking is how persistent are the beliefs in freedom despite violence, in progress in the face of the wedge of death.

There is no struggle between science and art or between evolutionary biology and spiritual faith; there *is* a constant struggle between the spirit of free inquiry and the spirit of fundamentalist dogma. That struggle is the story of human intellectual history. Atheism is no guarantee of humane conduct. Stalin and Hitler borrowed religious ideas, certainly, but they weren't believers. *Nothing* is any guarantee of humane conduct, except an insistence on it. In this sense, though Darwinism implies no politics, not even a liberal one, it does imply a philosophy. As the biologist Ernst Mayr wrote, it implies an intense awareness that all categorical or essentialist claims about living things are overdrawn— anyone who says that all cases of this thing or that thing are naturally one way or another is saying something that isn't so. It also teaches a great respect for the rule of variation, and the particular case. Mill's theory that eccentricity is necessary in society was intuitively closer to Darwin's theory of nature than the other grander theories. There are no neat lines between organisms. There are, truly, no straight lines in nature. The world is a gently graded blending of individual cases into apparent groups. Repetition is the habit of nature, but variation is the rule of life.

The liberal belief in the primacy of the single case is not an illusion nurtured by fancy but a hope quietly underscored—at a distance, pianissimo—by science. The general case is the tentative abstract hypothesis; the case right there is the real thing. This individualism is no guarantee of anything good. If we thought it better to treat people as though there *were* neat absolute lines between races, tribes, classes, and sexes, we could—and for most of human history, we have. If we would like to believe that humans are getting smarter, that evolution is inevitable, that progress is written into our very nature, that participatory democracy is a condition to which our genes for cooperation and altruism tend to lead us—well, there is nothing in a hundred thousand years of history to tell us that it's so. "Outraged nature" ought to rebound against tyranny, or cruelty, but it won't. Evolutionary theory can only say—and it's a lot—that if we want the rule of law, free speech, and individual rights, equality of races and sexes, there is nothing in biology to tell us that we can't.

Darwinism, and liberal science, is no threat to humane values and never has been. Yet there is a way in which the anxiety that so many people feel in the face of the primacy of science reflects something real and unalterable. There is something else, something deeper, and that is our awareness of the gap between our knowledge and our experience. The negotiation of that gap, more than any other single thing, is what marks the lives of this book's two subjects and the modern world they helped to create and we have inherited.

All science, all politics, is necessarily and always the aggregate of experience, while all of our actual experience is individual. Psychology studies children, tells us just how children learn, and traces all the patterns of development that children share, but as our children partake of the pattern, we don't think, "What a pattern!" We think, "What a kid!" All science is about graphs and charts and patterns on spectrums, and it tells immense amounts about how alike we are; all literature is about specific experience, and says that what happens only to us counts too.

We have common experiences and core experience, aggregate knowledge and individual notes. The common experience is that which we share with everyone else. We learn language at two, become sexually aware at twelve, get married at twenty, get bitter at forty, leave our partners at fifty, have a heart attack at sixty, and die at seventy. Your mileage may vary—if you're living on the savanna, you're maybe too healthy to have that heart attack, or else, more likely, you're dead already—but these are the norms.

Our core experience, on the other hand, is irreplaceably our own. Our children grow old, hit their developmental markers, become alert at thirteen months and angry at thirteen years— they hit twenty and want all the mates they can find and hit fifty and want a younger mate. All of it goes like clockwork, and all of it feels like chance. (The moment our core experience fits perfectly into the common experience is the moment we call rapture—when our children are born or the home team wins and the whole city celebrates. The moment when an account of individual experience touches the aggregated experience is the moment we call art.)

Lincoln and Darwin both knew this. They both had profound knowledge of the common experience of death—Lincoln, of death in war; Darwin, of death as the great sorter of existence— yet when death touched their core experience, that knowledge was of absolutely no help or consolation. Charles wouldn't have grieved less for Annie, or Mary for Willie, if they had known more about the vulnerability of small children to tuberculosis and typhoid. Annie was not one monkey among many, who could be replaced by some other young female of the same age and genetic constitution. Individual experience is not reducible to general laws, not because of some mysterious essence that defies scientific explanation but because the explanation, as Darwin saw, begins with the existence of the irreducible individual case.

That, again, is one central point of Darwinism. The habit of nature is regularity, but the rule of life is variation. No one had looked more grimly into the face of mass death than Abraham Lincoln, who grasped the awful arithmetic of modern war. But he could never detach himself from all that death, or find help in apprehension of the aggregate when death touched his own core. Darwin knew better than anyone that the wedge of death was inexorable, cleaving the quick from the lifeless without purpose or plan. But his knowledge didn't ease his grief when Annie died. Masterly knowledge of the common experience brought no understanding or consolation. All the attentions of his adult life had been devoted to this subject: the propagation and blind culling, the winnowing of each species' young on the threshing floor of death. No one understood this better than Charles Darwin; no one else understood it at that time *except* Charles Darwin. And it made no difference at all.

"And Now It's Happening to Me!"—it could be the title of an allegory of modern life. The space between the two kinds of experience has become the irony of our condition. The error of the scientifically minded is to think that objective truths about the common experience can temper the irrationalities brought on by the core experience; the error of the religionist is to think that the intensity of the core experience can negate objective truths about the common fate. Science lets us think big, but we still feel small. No cosmologist has ever felt more serenely about his tenure case by contemplating the vastness of the universe. We get the big picture, but it's not where we live.

People have always been unique in perceiving this gap, and in the knowledge of their mortality; the aggregate experience and our understanding of it make almost no difference to the individual experience and our experience of it. But in modern times, science has made that divide larger than it has ever been before. No one has ever put it better than Van Gogh, in the last of our little epigraphs at the beginning of this chapter, and the point he made is subtler than it may at first seem. It is true, certainly, he tells us, that the world is round, but that doesn't alter our experience of it as flat when we walk from central Paris to the suburb of Asnières. The world is round and feels flat; our lives are flat and feel round. The flatness we experience on foot is nonetheless real for being part of a round fact; the roundness we feel is no less dear for taking place on a flat plane. We live horizontally, still hoping ahead.

This is a truth that can't be explained, or explained away. It can only be asserted, as it can only be experienced. Most societies bound by tribe or religion bridge the space between the common and the core with ritual and dogma, and they do it successfully, for a while anyway. There's a beautiful poem by Yehuda Amichai about the Jewish prayer shawl that captures the profundity of this feeling so well:

Whoever put on a tallis when he was young will never forget:
taking it out of the soft velvet bag, opening the folded shawl,
spreading it out, kissing the length of the neckband (embroidered
or trimmed in gold). Then swinging it in a great swoop overhead
like a sky, a wedding canopy, a parachute. And then winding it
around his head as in hide-and-seek, wrapping
his whole body in it, close and slow, snuggling into it like the cocoon
of a butterfly, then opening would-be wings to fly.

For religious people, the snuggle and the flight are one. Individual experience feeds into the collective experience as a river flows into the ocean, and as the ocean makes the rain that makes the rivers. Living modern lives means that we don't want, or can't have, that simple comfort. Living a modern life means being "doubly conscious," as Herndon said that Lincoln was; it means being both the first of the moderns and the first of the anti-moderns, as Darwin's son said of his father. It means walking flat and living round, as Vincent insisted to Émile Bernard.

Both Lincoln and Darwin are princes of our disorder in this way, too, symptoms of the syndrome: they were family men but not social men. They lived lives that touched millions—and, in Lincoln's case, brought about the deaths of hundreds of thousands—but their lives were lived almost outside the traditional bounds of community. Lincoln was a politician with supporters and partners, but he had at most one or two real friends, and even they felt they never really knew him. Darwin, as his son knew, was of the same kind; if anything, they both retreated from the clan life, whether of the frontier or the British upper classes, into the family life of the great pan-national bourgeoisie.

The values of that doubly conscious class were called by Kenneth Clark "heroic materialism," the materialism that rose between the end of the Civil War and the onset of the First World War, the materialism of bridges and empires. Humane materialism might be a better name for it—the recognition that there is a space between what we know and what we feel, and that our lives have to be lived as best we can live them within that space. We are all at one level molecule, at another level monkeys, or at another, men, and all these at once.

Angels and ages, and both at once. The finest tunings of emotion are real, and the big indifferent waves of nature are real too. The splash and the tide both happen at the same time; from the pebble's point of view the splash is louder and the tide merely a background. The pebble's experience is smaller than the ocean's, but it is no less real. We each wear our hats differently on our heads, within a world of culture finely tuned and nuanced. Liberalism accepts a plurality of hats in order to arrive at a working majority of hearts. It asks us to accept a very broad range of radically different kinds and types of people, bringing them to live together. The proper limits of tolerance will remain unsure, but we all have a common interest in their being as broad as we can make them. Our souls are our own; our hats, the world's. Man is neither ape nor angel, but a creature of ages that allow him to be both.

Enchantment, Utopia, epiphany, sublime insight—the grand words of Romanticism are not Darwinian words. (In fact, they never occur anywhere in his writing.) *Slight, small, varied, struggle, helpful, hopeful, natural, selection, modification* (not *revolutionary change*)— these are the words of Darwinism, and they have become the words of liberalism. By giving us a new set of words, Darwin changed our minds.

And if we expand the set to include the words that Lincoln made part of the inheritance of liberal democracy? "Government of the people, by the people"; "with malice toward none; with charity for all"; "the law of religion"; "the mystic chords of memory"; "the better angels of our nature"; "full measure of devotion"; "the dogmas of the quiet past, are inadequate to the stormy present." The materialist certitudes and rationalist confidence of undiluted Enlightenment thought are absent—no "give me liberty, or give me death" or even "life, liberty, and the pursuit of happiness." But the arguments of law and observation aren't less eloquent than the rhetoric of honor and imagination once was, or less able to move us. They show that we can argue from evidence and still evoke ideals.

What all the first modern artists, from Whitman to van Gogh, have believed is that, for whatever reason, and however it came to be, we are capable of witnessing and experiencing the world as more than the sum of our instincts and appetites. Our altruism is not simply our appetites compounded; our appetites are not simply our altruism exposed. "Reason . . . must furnish all the materials for our future support and defense," Lincoln said, and reason alone can point us to its limits. We can argue about anything, even about the nature and meaning of our mysticisms. Clark called our liberal faith "heroic materialism" and said it wouldn't be enough. Humane materialism, or mystical materialism, is closer to it, and it remains the best we have. Intimations of the numinous may begin and end in us, but they are as real as descriptions of the natural; Sunday feelings are as real as Monday facts. On this point, Darwin and Lincoln, along with all the other poets of modern life, would have agreed. There *is* more to man than the breath in his body, if only the hat on his head, and the hope in his heart.

A BIBLIOGRAPHIC NOTE

Hundreds, no, thousands, of good books have been written about both of these men, their lives, and their work. I have read only some of them and have tried to keep the essay form pure and amateur in the right way by not overloading this book with scholarly machinery. However, I hope to have made my debts, enormous as they are, to original scholars pretty clear in the pages, where shout-outs are given as required, and hope that this note in addition will do double work— not only pointing to debts more clearly, but also, and just as important, helping readers go deeper into this material, to find original sources and more voices than just my own.

DARWIN

Any student of Darwin should begin with his own books. The four most important, *On the Origin of Species; The Descent of Man, and Selection in Relation to Sex; The Voyage of the H.M.S. "Beagle";* and *The Expression of the Emotions in Man and Animals*, are best available in E. O. Wilson's edition, *From So Simple a Beginning: The Four Great Books of Charles Darwin* (Norton, 2006). *The Autobiography of Charles Darwin* is just as important, and I like the Norton edition from 1969, completely restored, and with notes by his granddaughter. The most valuable resource for amateur Darwinians is http://darwin-online.org.uk/, which is placing the complete works of Darwin online.

The Cambridge University Press has sponsored the enormous, necessary, multivolume edition of Darwin's correspondence. It is available in useful, small editions, which I've often read with pleasure and drawn from at ease, particularly *Evolution: Selected Letters of Charles Darwin 1860–1870* (Frederick Burkhardt, Samantha Evans, Alison M. Pearn, eds., Cambridge University Press, 2008) and *Origins: Selected Letters of Charles Darwin, 1822–1859* (Frederick Burkhardt, ed., with a foreword by Stephen Jay Gould, Cambridge University Press, 2008). Even better, and one of the really golden books, is *Metaphysics, Materialism and the Evolution of Mind:The Early Writings of Charles Darwin* (Paul H. Barrett and Howard E. Gruber, eds., University of Chicago Press, 1980). (The notebooks from 1838 are also available now online.)

The standard biographies of Darwin, which I have read and reread with pleasure (though with occasional differences of interpretation) are Janet Browne's authoritative two volumes *Charles Darwin:Voyaging* (Princeton University Press, 1996) and *Charles Darwin: The Power of Place* (Princeton University Press, 2003) and Adrian Desmond and James Moore's *Darwin* (Penguin, 1992), a terrific read with a strong emphasis on the social history of Darwin's time as a key to his thought and its reception. The "domestic reading" of Annie, and her role in Darwin's life, we owe to Randal Keynes's *Darwin, His Daughter and Human Evolution* (Riverhead, 2002). I have drawn on all three of these texts for ideas and inspiration throughout. Gillian Beer's *Darwin's Plots* (Cambridge University Press, 1983) was a pioneering effort to place Darwin in a literary context, while Charles Kingsley's *The Water-Babies* (first published by Macmillan and Co. in 1863, then Penguin, 2008) is an entertaining postscript. David Dobbs's *Reef Madness: Charles Darwin, Alexander Agassiz, and the Meaning of Coral* (Pantheon, 2005) is a fascinating study of an unknown story of Darwin's theoretical mind, which I have drawn from with pleasure. Lyanda Lynn Haupt's *Pilgrim on the Great Bird Continent: The Importance of Everything and Other Lessons from Darwin's Lost Notebooks* (Little, Brown, 2006) was particularly revelatory on Darwin's relation to the amateur bird-breeders, and Jonathan Weiner's *The Beak of the Finch* (Knopf, 1994) is both a fine account of the birth of the theory and an explanation of its continuing power. (In a more specialized mode, Frank Sulloway's debunking of the old myth of evolution's birth can be found in his article "Darwin and His Finches:The Evolution of a Legend" in *Journal of the History of Biology* 15:1–53.)

Steve Jones's *Almost Like a Whale:The Origin of Species Updated* (Doubleday, 1999) is an extraordinary attempt to combine Darwin's original text with what has been learned since. The writings of Ernst Mayr, particularly his *The Growth of Biological Thought: Diversity, Evolution, and Inheritance* (Belknap Press, 1985), *Evolution and the Diversity of Life: Selected Essays* (Belknap Press, 1997), and *One Long Argument: Charles Darwin and the Genesis of Modern Evolutionary Thought* (Harvard University Press, 2007), as well as his introduction to the 1964 Harvard University Press edition of Darwin's *Origin,* have all been central to my own understanding of what Darwin really "means." (Many years ago, Kirk Varnedoe and I concluded our *High and Low: Modern Art and Popular Culture* with a quote from Mayr.) Mayr's emphasis on the revolutionary nature of Darwin's opposition to the "typos," and to essentialist thinking generally, is the bedrock of a philosophical approach to evolution.

No modern student of Darwin interpretation can do without the work of Daniel C. Dennett, particularly his *Darwin's Dangerous Idea* (Simon & Schuster, 1995), any more than she can do without the very different work of the late and much-lamented Stephen Jay Gould— recognizing that they represent two different readings of Darwin's life, work, and importance (though a student of both might suggest that the areas of agreement are larger than the arguers might always allow). Gould's collections of essays are all essential, but one might pick out, as having changed my own views of the world, his *The Panda's Thumb* (paperback edition, Norton, 1992) and *Ever Since Darwin* (Norton, 1992), while more ambitious students will want to try his daunting *The Structure of Evolutionary Theory* (Belknap, 2002). Richard Dawkins's own, very contrary views have also always been worth reading—see for instance his *Unweaving the Rainbow* (Penguin Press, 1998)—while Matt Ridley's books (for instance, his *Genome* [Fourth Estate, 1999]) have been an invaluable help to me.

The secondary "philosophical" literature, attempting to reconcile Darwin and the humanities, and evolutionary thought with questions of faith, is also enormous: let me single out David Quammen's *The Reluctant Mr. Darwin* (Norton, 2006) both as a brief life and an interpretation, George Levine's *Darwin Loves You* (Princeton University Press, 2008), Philip Kitcher's *Living with Darwin: Evolution, Design and the Future of Faith* (Oxford University Press, 2007), and, in a slightly different but humane key, Gerald Weissmann's *Darwin's Audubon* (Perseus, 1998).

As I finished this book, someone drew my attention to Stanley Edgar Hyman's long-out-of-print but worthwhile *The Tangled Bank: Darwin, Marx, Frazer and Freud as Imaginative Writers* (Atheneum, 1961), which has many fine things to say about Darwin's vocabulary, particularly his ever-balanced use of "beauty" and "fatal."

LINCOLN

The Darwin literature is merely immeasurable; the Lincoln literature is infinite. When you are already up to your armpits in it, you realize you have hardly dipped a toe. To single out some of the countless books worth reading: David Herbert Donald's *Lincoln* (Simon & Schuster, 1996) is standard, and so will be the newer version by Richard Carwardine, *Lincoln: A Life of Purpose and Power* (Knopf, 2006). The older lives of Lincoln include Carl Sandburg's *Abraham Lincoln: The Prairie Years, The War Years*, recently reprinted in a paperback edition (Harvest Books, 2002)—though long out of fashion, this was the first one many of us ever read, and a recent rereading didn't disappoint. His chapter on Lincoln's humor is worth the price of admission, and while the account of Lincoln's relationship with Ann Rutledge, of which Sandburg makes much, following Herndon, has long been mocked by academics, it has recently been restored to the story as at least a plausible possibility by Joshua Wolf Shenk in his provocative and stimulating *Lincoln's Melancholy* (Houghton Mifflin, 2005)—a reminder never to count out the poet's intuition in writing history. I have also drawn much on William C. Harris's *Lincoln's Rise to the Presidency* (University Press of Kansas, 2007), on *Lincoln's Virtues: An Ethical Biography* by William Lee Miller (Knopf, 2002), as well as on Daniel Mark Epstein's *The Lincolns: Portrait of a Marriage* (Ballantine, 2008).

An excellent collection of the newest lines in Lincoln lore can be found in *Lincoln Revisited* (John Y. Simon, Harold Holzer, Dawn Vogel, eds., Fordham University Press, 2007). Doris Kearns Goodwin's *Team of Rivals: The Political Genius of Abraham Lincoln* (Simon & Schuster, 2005) got me started on the Lincoln path, along with James L. Swanson's *Manhunt: The Twelve-Day Chase for Lincoln's Killer* (HarperCollins, 2006) and Jay Winik's *April, 1865: The Month That Saved America* (HarperCollins, 2001). Both Goodwin and Winik spoke to me at length about their work, and I thank them for that. Lincoln's own speeches and writings are also best available now in a multivolume series from the Library of America.

My own thoughts on Lincoln's Lyceum address, and the code of honor, were first expressed at the Oxford University Press and New York Public Library lectures, on the romance of violence in America, which I gave in New York in the spring of 1995 but, for various reasons, have never published. Kenneth S. Greenberg's *Honor & Slavery* (Princeton University Press, 1996) is a superb discussion of the subject. David S. Reynolds's *John Brown, Abolitionist* (Knopf, 2005) was the occasion for a long review of my own in *The New Yorker,* which I have borrowed from for this book. I learned from every page, as I did from John Stauffer's *The Black Hearts of Men* (Harvard University Press, 2002).

On Lincoln's words and rhetoric, everyone begins with Garry Wills's *Lincoln at Gettysburg* (Touchstone, 1992). I have also been influenced by Van Wyck Brooks on Lincoln in his *The Times of Melville & Whitman* (Dutton, 1947), by Edmund Wilson's *Patriotic Gore* (Oxford University Press, 1962), and by Alfred Kazin's *God and the American Writer* (Knopf, 1997). Harold Holzer's *Lincoln at Cooper Union* (Simon & Schuster, 2004) is indispensable, as is *Lincoln's Sword* by Douglas L. Wilson (Knopf, 2006). Fred Kaplan's *Lincoln: The Biography of a Writer* (HarperCollins, 2008), which seems full of insight, appeared just after this book was finished. And, for the context of a rhetorical society, one should see also *The Age of Lincoln* by Orville Vernon Burton (Hill & Wang, 2007).

On Lincoln and the law, see Julie M. Fenster's *The Case of Abraham Lincoln* (Palgrave, 2007) and Brian Dirck's *Lincoln the Lawyer* (University of Illinois Press, 2007). On the Civil War, and its profound transformation of mourning and feeling, I have obviously been much influenced by Drew Gilpin Faust's *This Republic of Suffering: Death and the American Civil War* (Knopf, 2008), which I wrote about at length in *The New Yorker,* as well as by *Awaiting the Heavenly Country: The Civil War and America's Culture of Death* (Cornell University Press, 2008) by Mark S. Schantz. On Lincoln, slavery, and racism, and his relations with Frederick Douglass, see James Oakes, *The Radical and the Republican* (Norton, 2007) and John Stauffer, *Giants: The Parallel Lives of Frederick Douglass & Abraham Lincoln* (Twelve Books, 2008). On Lincoln at the Soldiers' Home, see *Lincoln's Sanctuary* by Matthew Pinsker (Oxford University Press, 2003). On Lincoln and Shakespeare, I'm grateful to conversations with John Andrews, who promises a book on

Shakespeare and the Lincoln assassination, as well as with Barry Edel-stein, Stephen Greenblatt, Tony Kushner, and Ramie Targoff. Alison Gopnik and Andrew Meltzoff's work on the invention of theory and the making of the human mind can be found in their books, most notably *Words, Thoughts and Theories* (MIT Press, 1997).

Finally, let me mark my debt, in the conclusion particularly but really throughout, to the writings of the two pillars of modern liberal thinking: Karl Popper's *The Open Society and Its Enemies* (Routledge and Kegan Paul, 1946) as well as his *Conjectures and Refutations: The Growth of Scientific Knowledge* (Routledge and Kegan Paul, 1963) and to the collected works of John Stuart Mill, available at length in any library. Intriguingly, both Popper and Mill were Darwinian skeptics of a modest kind—Mill not sure it could be so, Popper not sure that evo-lutionary theory was science in the sense that physics was science. A good reminder that great minds don't think alike and also that, as all three men knew, there is nothing like an argument.

My personal thanks also go especially to Harold Holzer, my guide into the Lincoln world, and to Daniel Dennett, who read my pages on Darwin, as well as to Frank Sulloway. Obviously, all faults remaining are mine. My debts to David Remnick, for his friendship and counsel, as well as to Ann Goldstein, and Peter Canby and his fact-checking team at *The New Yorker* are constant, as they are to Lydia Buechler and Lily Evans at Knopf. It was my intention to maintain the original tone of these chapters as more or less conversational *New Yorker* essays, more talk than thunder, by not overburdening them with apparatus and mechanics while still fine-tuning them for accuracy. I thank with all my heart Sophia Sherry, who tirelessly and charmingly checked and checked again all that was new in this book; the mistakes made, of which I'm sure there are some, are mine.

Conversations—on science, humanism, the drama of Darwin's life and of American history, and all their many and different discontents—with the late and ever-missed Kirk Varnedoe; Bernard Avishai; Malcolm Gladwell; my sister Alison Gopnik; my brother Blake Gop-nik; Stephen Gaghan; and, particularly, with Louis Menand have illu-minated many nights and mornings and shine on many pages. My friend and editor George Andreou persuaded me that a book on these subjects made sense, after the omniscient and omnivorous Henry Finder had first persuaded me to try and make sense of these subjects. I thank them both.

And Martha, constant reader and conscience! Of course, and the children, Luke and Olivia, the best free apps I have ever downloaded. Angels always, and now for ages.